Praise for
The Chief Development Offi

"With *The Chief Development Officer: Beyond Fundraising*, Ronald J. Schiller debunks stereotypes and assumptions about good development leaders and shares characteristics of the most successful chief development officers based on real-life experience and interviews. This should be required reading for any CEO or board chair hiring a new CDO and for any aspiring development officer who thinks he or she wants the job." —**Elizabeth Boluch Wood**, vice president for development, Princeton University

"The role of the chief development officer has expanded greatly over the past two decades, and Ron Schiller draws on his experience as a CDO and extensive research to offer sound advice to those taking on that role and those hiring a CDO. His examples of how CDOs excel or fall short can assist nonprofit organizations in making wise choices when it comes to filling this crucial position." —**Robert J. Zimmer**, president, University of Chicago

"Schiller has remarkable insight into the role of the chief development officer and cuts right through the rhetoric to get to the core of what leads to success." —**Jerry May**, vice president for development, University of Michigan

The Chief Development Officer

Beyond Fundraising

Ronald J. Schiller

ROWMAN & LITTLEFIELD EDUCATION
A division of
ROWMAN & LITTLEFIELD
Lanham • Boulder • New York • Toronto • Plymouth, UK

Published by Rowman & Littlefield Education
A division of Rowman & Littlefield
4501 Forbes Boulevard, Suite 200, Lanham, Maryland 20706
www.rowman.com

10 Thornbury Road, Plymouth PL6 7PP, United Kingdom

British Library Cataloguing-in-Publication Information Available

Library of Congress Cataloging-in-Publication Data Available

Schiller, Ronald J.
The chief development officer : beyond fundraising / by Ronald J. Schiller.
p. cm.
ISBN 978-1-61048-934-8 (cloth : alk. paper) — ISBN 978-1-61048-935-5 (pbk. : alk. paper) —
ISBN 978-1-61048-936-2 (electronic)

™ The paper used in this publication meets the minimum requirements of American
National Standard for Information Sciences Permanence of Paper for Printed Library
Materials, ANSI/NISO Z39.48-1992.

Printed in the United States of America

Contents

Contents

Foreword

A new president is selected, begins to settle into her office, and starts formulating the priorities that will launch her term with hope and excitement. She quickly learns, upon deeper examination, where, unbeknownst to her, additional strengths lie; she also realizes, inevitably, where the soft spots are softer than at first apparent. These revelations alter the areas demanding her early attention, changing the list substantially. Quickly, an assessment of the quality of advancement comes under her lens because she knows she must consider, organize, and then commence a capital campaign if the aspirations of the institution are to become attainable. Many times, in these circumstances, the decision to seek new leadership is made and the search process begins.

Ron Schiller's book is not a blueprint for how to conduct a search. Rather, it is an in-depth discussion of what to look for in a chief development officer, who must be not only a trusted colleague, but also an effective thought leader, an organizational expert, a psychologist, a cheerleader, a mentor, and a magnet for talent and potential talent, all applied with the optimism of a rookie and the wisdom of a veteran.

As I read it, the objective of this book is to elevate the entire profession by eliminating missteps that organization after organization seem to make. In today's world, an erroneous selection can mean a decade of decline that will take another decade to reverse.

There are many "how-to" books on the mechanics of fundraising, and they make important contributions. However, one of the revealing tendencies Ron has discovered through extensive interviews with presidents and trustees is that the majority of firings of chief development officers are not due to an inability to raise money. The changes are made because of an inability to relate effectively to the many, many constituencies within and outside the institution. As Ron points out, the very first on that list is the chemistry between the chief development officer and the president. Success here depends on the soft skills that determine how we come across to those we meet and want to make stakeholders in our institutions. Steven M. C. Covey wrote a book entitled *The Speed of Trust: The One Thing That Changes Everything.* It takes us partway in developing the understanding we seek, a very valuable contribution. Ron's book builds on the premises I found in Covey's book in that it applies the principles specifically to the world of development.

Let me suggest an example from my own experience. When asking each person in a group to give a one-word description of someone he or she admires greatly, we learn something about how we may be perceived. Let us say there are 30 people in the group and each of their words is written on a board and then put into one of three categories: a gift, a learned skill, or an attitude. A gift might be that a basketball player is seven feet tall, a learned skill would be that he can go either left or right with equal effectiveness, and an attitude is that he seeks to be supportive of his teammates at all times.

Some of the words we hear are respectful, kind, trustworthy, affirming, encouraging, supportive, fair, genuine, caring, thoughtful, perceptive, or attentive. When we place the descriptors into our categories, I have found that at least 75 percent are in the attitude column. They are what I call soft skills as contrasted with the learned skills of the basketball player.

Ron's book is filled with insights on how we might judge in advance whether a person can cope and make contributions in discussions representing multiple demands from multiple constituencies in multiple settings. It also contains insights on how long-term relationships are built, the relationships that result in lifelong support of our institutions while building trust within the academic community.

This work adds a dimension of understanding of the demands of the development profession I have never seen articulated in my 40-plus years of engagement in our work. I will suggest it to presidents, to trustees, to every search committee, and to every professional who believes advancement is his or her path to a satisfying life of work.

Curtis R. Simic
President Emeritus, Indiana University Foundation

Preface

The Chief Development Officer: Beyond Fundraising draws on my experience in the roles of chief development officer (CDO), board member, and fundraising consultant. It also draws on my current work with chief executive officers (CEOs) and other nonprofit leaders in my role as founding partner of the Aspen Leadership Group, a national executive search and consulting firm focused exclusively on the social profit sector.

During 25 years in frontline fundraising and fundraising leadership positions, I saw the role of CDO expand significantly. Through my work in search, I have observed more broadly the impact of this expansion on the success rate and tenure of CDOs. Board members, CEOs, consultants, and development officers all confirmed the need for assistance in understanding how and why the role has evolved and the competencies required for success in the role today.

"CDO," for the purposes of this book, is defined as the most senior staff member charged with development/fundraising responsibilities in a nonprofit organization. The CDO reports directly to the CEO in virtually every nonprofit organization. The most common titles for the CDO are

- Senior Vice President for Development (or Advancement, or Development and Communications, or Alumni Relations and Development)
- Vice President for Development (or Advancement, or Development and Communications, or Alumni Relations and Development)
- Vice Chancellor for Development (or Advancement, or Development and Communications, or Alumni Relations and Development)
- Chief Development Officer
- Chief Advancement Officer
- Executive Director of Development

- Director of Development
- President of the Foundation (usually at a public nonprofit with a related foundation responsible for fundraising)
- Executive Director of the Foundation

Research for this book included interviews with 69 nonprofit leaders: CEOs, board members, development consultants, and CDOs. A list of those interviewed will be found in Appendix E. Collectively, the CDOs interviewed have served in the role of CDO 86 times. The CEOs, board members, and consultants interviewed have collectively worked with hundreds of CDOs. I asked each interviewee the following questions:

- How many CDOs have you supervised/how many CDO roles have you held/with how many CDOs have you worked?
- How many of these CDOs reported directly to the CEO?
- Were the CDOs in what the CEOs would consider their "inner cabinet"?
- To your knowledge, was the CDO's predecessor asked or encouraged to step down?
- Do you know of other CDOs who were asked or encouraged to step down?
- If so, what were the main reasons?
- Would you say that any or all of the CDOs asked to step down were competent frontline fundraisers?
- Thinking of the most successful CDO you have known, or thinking of the "ideal" CDO (who might be a composite of two or three of the most successful CDOs you have known), what are the competencies that most distinguished that individual?
- Thinking of the weakest CDO you have known, what key competencies was he or she missing? In other words, in what required roles/responsibilities did he or she not excel?
- What percentage of time does your CDO/do you as CDO/do the CDOs you work with spend on direct fundraising and fundraising program management?
- If you were hiring me to fill a CDO position reporting to you, what two or three competencies would you consider to be the most important for my success in working with you?
- What advice would you give to a roomful of aspiring CDOs?

I also asked for stories and anecdotes that illustrate what presidents and board chairs most need from today's CDO, what officers and consultants have observed in the most and least successful CDOs, and what leading CDOs consider to be the most critical elements in the preparation of aspiring

CDOs. I also asked each person for three "words of wisdom" he or she would pass along to aspiring CDOs.

The Chief Development Officer: Beyond Fundraising is a guide not only to those preparing for the role of CDO but also to those charged with selecting, appointing, and supporting CDOs. It includes nine chapters, each presenting a role beyond frontline fundraising and fundraising program management in which today's top CDOs excel:

- Relationship Builder in Chief
- Shaper of Culture That Embraces Philanthropic Partnership
- Strategist and Planner
- Trusted Advisor on Board Matters
- Thought Partner
- Flag Bearer
- Visionary and Confident Sight Raiser
- Talent Magnet
- Mentor to Future CDOs

Each chapter includes a description of the elements of the role, illustrations of how CDOs excel, and advice on preparing for the role. The book concludes with suggestions on what individuals can do, what organizations can do, and what the profession can do to help CDOs succeed; some words of wisdom to aspiring CDOs; a hiring guide; and suggestions for CDO candidates.

For years, I've observed to colleagues that there are many wonderful development leaders and a lot of wonderful nonprofit organizations, but not always the best "marriages" between leaders and organizations. The immediate goal of this book is better "marriages," leading to an ultimate goal of continued health and growth of nonprofit organizations and the essential contributions they make to a civil society.

Acknowledgments

When I began my career in fundraising, the most common question at gatherings of development professionals was, "What did you do before you got into fundraising?" My story, like so many others, involved an "accident" rather than a career plan conceived during college years. Several years later, hearing me tell someone how I "fell into" fundraising, my mother gently corrected me, reminding me that I had been a fundraiser since elementary school. I hadn't thought of the skate-a-thon to raise money for the new high school gym, or the pizza sales to fund a class trip, in many years.

So I begin my acknowledgments with my parents. My mother has taught me more about sight raising than any other person, and my father is the consummate relationship builder. They both launched my career in fundraising, supporting me cheerfully and tirelessly through dozens of fundraising activities throughout my childhood.

The idea for the book stemmed from discussions with my friend and colleague of many years Lois L. Lindauer, founder and CEO of Lois L. Lindauer Searches, a leading development search firm.

From its conception, Susan Feagin, Trish Jackson, Sue Paresky, Robert Sharpe, Jim Thompson, Bob Zimmer, and especially Curt Simic provided encouragement and great enthusiasm. I'm indebted to them and to other generous readers including Suzanne Baker, Tim Child, Rebecca Smith, and David Unruh.

Kate Lunde and Jeff Hanavan spent countless hours bringing fresh eyes and thoughtful restructuring to the final draft.

Nancy Evans and Caitlin Crawford of Rowman & Littlefield were immediately enthusiastic about the project and tremendously supportive throughout the publication process.

Unwavering support for this book came, as it comes each day in every aspect of my life, from my life partner, Alan Fletcher. This, my first book, is dedicated to him.

Introduction

The Evolving Role of Chief Development Officer

Until recently, the chief development officer (CDO) in nonprofit organizations has focused primarily if not exclusively on fundraising. In the past two decades, the roles, responsibilities, and corresponding required competencies of CDOs have evolved, and they will continue to expand *beyond* fundraising.

PRINCIPAL DRIVERS OF EVOLUTION IN THE ROLE

Greater need combined with greater competition for philanthropic dollars has changed the role of CEOs, the expectations of boards, and the importance of fundraising in the overall management and strategic direction of nonprofit organizations. As a result, CDOs play a more senior leadership role than ever before.

Greater Demand for Revenue

In a weak economy, organizations experience an unsurprising increase in the need for private support, due to

- reductions in earned income;
- losses in endowment and corresponding reductions in endowment income;
- changes in government support; and
- increased demand for services provided by the nonprofit.

In a strong economy, however, organizations make bold, visionary plans that also increase demand for fundraising. These plans include new and expanded programs, new and renovated facilities, and increased long-term financial stability through additions to endowment.

In short, demand for fundraising revenue grows whether the economy is weak or strong.

Increasing Competition

The number of registered 501(c)(3) organizations—public charities—in the United States increased from 1.26 million in 2001 to 1.57 million in 2011, 25 percent in that decade alone. According to the Urban Institute, "The growth rate of the nonprofit sector has surpassed the rate of both the business and government sectors."[1]

This growth, combined with greater demand for fundraising revenue, has resulted in increased competition for

- board members with capacity to provide leadership and financial resources;
- high-quality administrative and programmatic leaders;
- high-performing staff members;
- "consumers" such as audience members, patients, and students; and
- philanthropic dollars.

Fundraising and voluntarism are also expanding internationally. Many organizations overseas look to the United States, with a firmly established culture of philanthropy, as a source of potential donors and development officers. A growing number of U.S. organizations are raising money from donors across the globe.

Greater Reliance on Board Members

Board members have always played a critical role in fundraising. With a growing number of nonprofit competitors, and with larger and larger campaigns, organizations rely more than ever on board members to provide many of the largest gifts in annual giving campaigns as well as in capital campaigns. Nationwide, of the largest gifts made by individuals each year, consistently more than half, sometimes almost all, are from governing or advisory board members or founders of the organizations that benefited from these gifts.

In addition to personal giving, fundraising leadership of board members also must include willingness, at least on the part of some, to assist in raising money from others. Top CDOs are experts in working directly with board members and in supporting board interactions of colleagues, especially CEOs.

Shifts in the Role and Responsibilities of the Chief Executive Officer

Greater demand for fundraising revenue and increased expectations of board members have led to changes in the role of the CEO. In recruiting CEOs, boards routinely put a premium on fundraising talent, skill, and passion. When CEOs retire, their fundraising record is always highlighted, often in the first sentence. The amount of time and energy that CEOs focus on fund-raising varies widely: In hospitals with separate foundations responsible for fundraising, CEOs may spend only 10 percent of their time on fundraising; in small arts or social services organizations, CEOs may spend 60 percent or more of their time on fundraising. In all nonprofits, CEOs rely more than ever on their CDOs—for advice, counsel, expertise, and partnership in work that increasingly determines whether CEOs are seen as successful.

TODAY'S CDO

The role of CDO is one of the most exhilarating, challenging, and rewarding roles in the nonprofit world. Philanthropists are extraordinary people, with fascinating stories, doing marvelous things. Nonprofits continue to make critically important contributions to society, adapting and responding to new challenges and opportunities.

At the same time, greater demand for fundraising revenue, increasing competition, elevated expectations of board members, and changes in the role of CEO require new skills and approaches. "Things have changed. Stresses are different. Size of development programs is different. Competition is different. Reliance on private revenue is greater. Because of that, CDOs have to change," says Susan Paresky, senior vice president for development at Dana-Farber Cancer Institute.

Fundraising Is Only Part of the Job

CDOs are and have always been expected to be excellent frontline fundrais-ers and fundraising strategists. What is different today is that most CDOs devote less than half of their time to direct fundraising—some report as little as 10 percent. Matthew Eynon, named vice president for advancement at Franklin & Marshall College in 2012, jokes that he spends "75 percent of my time on fundraising and 75 percent on everything else!" New CDOs easily relate: They must devote considerable time and attention, early in their ten-ures, to anchoring themselves as credible organizational leaders.

In fundraising programs large and small, whether CDOs spend 10 percent or 60 percent of their time on fundraising, other responsibilities associated with being senior organizational officers, reporting directly to CEOs, require significant time and attention. "CDOs and their organizations need to realize that the job of CDO is very different from the job of frontline fundraiser or mid-level fundraising manager," says Susan Washburn, principal, Washburn & McGoldrick. "CDOs who aren't prepared to serve as a member of the CEO's cabinet in the role of senior organizational officer go off the rails, either by chest-beating and trying to prove they know what they're doing, or by becoming quickly overwhelmed or intimidated."

One board chair, who has worked with seven CDOs, says, "In a small development office, fundraising skill in the CDO is essential. But in a big organization, though the CDO is still accountable for fundraising results, fundraising skill has almost become 'nice to have' more than 'critical.' It is not nearly as important as leadership and strategic partnership skills." Cecile Richards, president of Planned Parenthood Federation of America and Planned Parenthood Action Fund, agrees: "The ability to bring discipline, strategic thinking, and long-range vision, combined with the ability to deploy staff, board members, and the CEO in an effective fashion, is more important to me than experience and ability as a frontline fundraiser."

Each organization has different requirements, and CDOs as well as their bosses need to find the right balance between direct fundraising and other responsibilities, in order to permit CDOs to make the most significant contribution possible. Requirements will vary according to

- the extent of growth or change that is required in the fundraising staff and program;
- the degree to which the CEO and board members are engaged in fundraising; and
- the qualities required to complement the CEO and other members of the organization's senior leadership.

Requirements will also change over time. Accepting other roles and responsibilities as part of the job rather than as distractions from fundraising allows CEOs and CDOs to set and meet more clearly stated and widely embraced expectations.

As senior leaders, CDOs need a structure that allows them to manage up, sideways, and down at the same time. The ability to hire great people, especially direct reports, and empower them for success is essential. "Delegating is more important than ever; CDOs have to build strong teams and trust them," says Karl Clauss, vice president for development and alumni relations at Swarthmore College. "Talent magnet" was second only to "relationship builder" in importance to the success of today's CDO, among those interviewed.

CDOs Are Senior Officers

As senior officers of their organizations, today's CDOs contribute to many areas beyond fundraising, including

- governance;
- finance, budgeting, and investments;
- communications, marketing, and branding;
- strategic and long-term planning;
- enrollment management, audience development, or membership;
- government and community relations;
- technology;
- crisis management; and
- legal affairs.

In addition, CDOs must be masters of diplomacy, balancing the various and sometimes competing interests and priorities of many constituents and stakeholders, including

- board leaders and members;
- the CEO;
- colleagues who report to the CEO;
- staff with significant responsibility and power within the organization;
- donors and potential donors;
- participants and beneficiaries, such as audience members, patients, and alumni; and
- volunteers and volunteer leaders.

Involved and visible in every part of their organizations, CDOs gain broad perspective, strengthening their capacity to serve as strategic thought partners to administrative and board leaders. They have unparalleled access to the board, regular interaction with every senior leader of the organization, and CEOs who today devote much if not most of their own time to fundraising. Excellent chemistry and alignment with CEOs and preparation to function as one of the principal leaders of an organization as a whole have become more important for the CDO than ever.

Their organizational leadership roles help them and their teams produce fundraising results with much greater impact. "CDOs who accept larger organizational leadership responsibility avoid the trap of pressing ideas that might work for fundraising but are not wholly congruent with the needs and values of the organization," says Don Randel, president of the Andrew W. Mellon Foundation.

Turnover at the Level of CDO

The 69 people interviewed were collectively aware of over 200 CDOs who have been asked or encouraged to step down. Consultants who work with dozens of CDOs and nonprofit organizations consistently reported that CDOs are more often and more frequently being asked to step down. CDOs interviewed, collectively, have held 86 CDO roles; in at least 53 of these roles their predecessor had been asked to step down. Many of those interviewed had seen at least one CDO come and go within a year, even in the most highly regarded fundraising programs. Several of those interviewed had been asked to step down themselves.

In early 2013, CompassPoint Nonprofit Services and the Evelyn and Walter Haas, Jr. Fund released the results of a study involving more than 2,700 development directors and charity heads. In the foreword to the report, Linda Wood, Senior Director, Leadership and Grantmaking at the Evelyn and Walter Haas, Jr. Fund, writes, "Our survey data confirm that many of the fundraising challenges facing nonprofits today can be traced to high turnover and other problems in the development director position."[2]

"Performance expectations defined in financial terms alone deny the reality of what it takes to get givers, not just gifts," concludes the report. It suggests that expectations of the CDO include "contribution to the vision, strategy, and overall leadership of an organization." One sign that an organization has created an environment for success is that "the development director is viewed as a key leader and partner in the organization and is integrally involved in organizational planning and strategy."[3]

Superb Fundraising Ability Is Not Enough

Most of the CDOs known to have been asked to step down were, in the words of interviewees, "very good," "excellent," and even "superb" fundraisers. CEOs, board chairs, CDOs, and consultants consistently confirmed two principal reasons for transition in the role of CDO:

- weak partnerships between CDOs and CEOs or other senior leaders; and
- inability or perceived inability to contribute to overall leadership of the organization.

In most nonprofit organizations, the CDO is one of the two or three most important advisors to the CEO, and their partnership requires excellent chemistry, shared values, and enormous trust. Nearly every CDO competency identified as critical by those interviewed has a significant impact on the CEO-CDO relationship. A superlative relationship creates a much stronger platform for fundraising.

Consultants and leading development professionals across the nation and in all nonprofit sectors—education, health care, the arts, and social services—agreed that CDOs as well as those who hire them need a more comprehensive understanding of the role. Aspiring CDOs would benefit from expanded training and opportunity to gain broader skills and experiences. A better understanding of the role would clarify expectations of everyone involved in the hiring and support of CDOs, improving the likelihood that the right person is in the right place at the right time. One thing is clear: The number of zeros on a resume, in millions or billions raised, is not by itself a predictor of success in the role.

The Cabinet within the Cabinet

"The role is a broad institutional leadership role," says Ann McLaughlin Korologos, former U.S. Secretary of Labor and chair of multiple boards. "CDOs need broader talents and should be prepared to be players in the running of the business of their organizations." CDOs increasingly serve, in the words of one college president, as "members of the cabinet within the cabinet."

SUMMARY

The role is not for everyone. Aspiring CDOs need better information to determine whether the role is right for them, along with guidance in choosing the right organizations to serve and the right challenges to embrace. CEOs and board members need better information to guide their hiring decisions and to create environments more conducive to CDO success.

Much is written on the subject of CDO turnover. But turnover is not inherently bad; a certain amount of turnover is healthy and is essential to growth. And focusing on the negative may illuminate a problem, but it rarely leads to productive change.

There are challenges in the role and its evolution, to be sure. For some, these changes make the role more appealing. "The job is much more challenging and complex today than even a few years ago, but for the right person, it's a more interesting job as a result," says Cecile Richards.

Thousands of CDOs are thriving, and many of their programs experience little staff turnover. Dozens of CDOs interviewed have served in the role for years, and many for decades, and they wouldn't trade it for any other. "Over the 35 years of my career, I have enjoyed this profession beyond my wildest expectations," says Mark Kostegan, senior vice president for development, Mount Sinai Hospital. "I have partnered with scores of volunteer leaders, caregivers, and philanthropists in helping to advance critically important work. How tremendously rewarding it is!"

The following pages describe the roles and responsibilities of today's CDO with examples from across the nonprofit sector. They highlight competencies and approaches that distinguish today's successful CDO—beyond fundraising.

NOTES

1. Urban Institute, www.urban.org/nonprofits/index.cfm.
2. Jeanne Bell and Marla Cornelius, *Underdeveloped* (CompassPoint and Evelyn and Walter Haas, Jr. Fund, 2013), 2.
3. Bell and Cornelius, *Underdeveloped*, 11, 26.

Chapter One

Relationship Builder in Chief

Virtually every person associated with a nonprofit organization—employee, volunteer, beneficiary, or donor—has a vested interest in the success of that organization's fundraising program and therefore high expectations for its CDO and development staff. Each of these individuals has a unique responsibility, a unique perspective, and associated fundraising hopes and demands, and CDOs interact with nearly all of them. In an environment where there are never enough resources to satisfy each and every need and desire, competent CDOs remember that all are trying to do their best for their organizations.

In addition to CEOs, executive staff members, development staff members, board members, and other donors and volunteers, CDOs regularly interact with

- department leaders such as deans, or chairs of departments, or artistic directors;
- leading faculty members, artists, or physicians;
- staff members in other parts of the organization;
- investment advisors, attorneys, and other donor representatives;
- community leaders, including legislators and local business owners;
- consultants, including executive search consultants, leadership and staff development consultants, campaign consultants, governance experts, prospect research experts, auditors, and technology consultants;
- students, alumni, audience members, subscribers, patients, and other beneficiaries or consumers; and
- parents, grandparents, family members of patients, and others touched by the organization.

Knowing the priorities of such a variety of constituents, and recognizing the expertise, perspective, and financial resources each brings to the table, CDOs are in an exceptional position to build strong relationships that will advance an organization's mission, facilitate synergy, and minimize contention. "CDOs approach constituents like family members at a Thanksgiving dinner," says one CDO. "You don't necessarily like everyone at the table, and you expect that some people will carry on, saying or doing things that upset others. Because you understand who they are and how they think, you are in a position to know what they really mean, and you can anticipate how they will react. You are prepared to remain publicly nonjudgmental. Your primary focus is on keeping the relationship going over time."

Susan Paresky adds, "Being a great personal relationship-builder is key, but it is not enough. When the CDO leaves, personal relationships must continue. The CDO is responsible for building development program relationships and organizational relationships that are sustainable. If the strength of relationships rests only with the CDO, they've failed the organization."

As senior officers, the relationships they build, as well as those they facilitate between colleagues and donors, extend beyond fundraising. "When CDOs build effective relationships for their organizations, board members and donors know they can call them about anything," says Deborah Breen, president of the Aspen Valley Hospital Foundation. "Those CDOs also know that relationships don't end with a gift; a gift is only the beginning."

"People give to people," a common expression in the development profession, applies not only to gifts of money but also to gifts of time and goodwill: *We support those we like and respect.* Effective CDOs are consistently described as good-natured, approachable, and patient, with a healthy sense of humor. Masters of diplomacy, they rise above conflict and competition and guide colleagues through tense situations while keeping relationships healthy and intact. As priorities evolve, and as leaders change, these CDOs remain relentlessly positive, investing daily in renewing and strengthening relationships and in keeping colleagues unified and energized, even when solutions don't go as hoped or when communication temporarily breaks down.

THE CDO'S MOST IMPORTANT RELATIONSHIP: THE CEO

An excellent partnership with the CEO is vital to organizational fundraising success, and it is *essential* to CDO job security. CDOs recognize the paramount importance of this relationship, investing great care in establishing and maintaining absolute and mutual trust, respect, and confidence. A board chair put it this way: "The CDO has to vibrate on the same frequency as the

CEO. It helps if this is true of other senior officers, but it *must* be true of the CDO."

CEOs expect their CDOs to provide regular updates on fundraising activity—in meetings, one-on-one, by e-mail, and by whatever other means of communication the CEOs prefer—and to be able to answer any and all questions related to that activity. They rely on CDOs for

- advice on relationships with individual board members and top donors, related to and beyond fundraising;
- knowledge of the organization and its work sufficient to make meaningful contributions to strategic planning discussions;
- thought partnership in shaping vision and strategies around large, transformational gift opportunities;
- assistance in preparing for speeches, presentations, meetings, and other interactions with key volunteer and donor constituencies;
- honesty at all times: when there's news that's hard to deliver, CDOs get it right and deliver it promptly; and
- excellent judgment in the use of CEO time.

In addition, they assume CDOs will

- maintain productive relationships with other executive staff members;
- master best practices in the development profession, including the appropriate adaptation and application of them; and
- maintain an understanding of the competitive landscape for raising funds in their organization's community, region, and, when applicable, across the nation.

Confidence and Trust between CEO and CDO

CEOs must have complete confidence in their CDO partners. Loss of this inevitably leads to CDO departures and is a leading cause of transition in the position of CDO: In the 200 CDO transitions observed by those interviewed, loss of CEO confidence played a role in more than 90 percent of departures. "The basic problem was a disconnect between our CEO and CDO, and that led to a yawning chasm of distrust," said a CDO's direct report, describing the events leading up to her CDO being asked to step down. "With the CDO always feeling second-guessed by the CEO, everything around and under the CDO started to fracture."

The successful CDO has the confidence of other senior leaders as well. When it is lacking, the situation may become fatal for CDOs, especially if CEOs are forced to devote precious time and energy to mediating or working around weak or damaged CDO relationships. One trustee described a situation in which the CEO had to ask a CDO to step down due to an irreparable relationship between the CDO and the board chair, even though "the relationship between the CEO and CDO was excellent." A CEO in higher education spoke of a former CDO who "wanted complete control of everything related to development." The CDO "made it clear in executive staff meetings, both verbally and through his body language, that he was not interested in the business of other units, and that other executive staff members should run their own units and leave him alone to run development."

CDOs generally have greater access to CEOs than most or all of their colleagues. James Cuno, president and CEO of the J. Paul Getty Trust, points out that "CDOs enjoy a constant and very close relationship with the CEO, traveling together, spending many evenings together over dinner with donors, and discussing relationships with some of the organization's most important and influential volunteer leaders." This close relationship requires CDOs to pay even greater attention to integration with other members of the leadership team, to avoid any suggestion that the CDO's relationship with the CEO is more important than that of other senior officers. "The CDO must develop a very close relationship but not at the expense of the chemistry of the whole senior team."

Some CEOs joked that they spend almost as much time with their CDOs as with their spouses. CDOs talked about the similarities between managing relationships with CEOs and managing relationships with life partners, especially in terms of maintaining the highest levels of trust and confidence. One CEO observed that when a provost is a finalist in a presidential search for another college or university, the provost's cachet in his or her home institution usually rises, but when a CDO is in another search, the CEO and other organizational leaders feel betrayed. In fact, numerous CDOs pointed to colleagues who lost their jobs in part due to such a perceived betrayal.

CEOs need to be confident that CDOs are wholly committed to their vision. CDOs sometimes inadvertently contribute to loss of confidence by "crushing the dream"—responding to aspirations of CEOs and other senior leaders without the enthusiasm they expect. Reactions intended to be realistic may come across as pessimistic or dismissive. Enterprising leaders realize that not every dream can become a reality. Yet they neither need nor want their CDOs to be among the first doubters. By studying the feasibility of an idea and presenting thoughtful analysis in a spirit of "getting to yes," effective CDOs enable leaders to decide for themselves whether an idea is realistic. CEOs understandably grow to resent CDOs who jump to a conclusion ahead of them.

CDOs in turn want to have confidence in their CEOs. In order to do their best work, they need CEOs who are not just visionary, respected, and engaging, but also willing, able, and supportive fundraising partners. A CDO recently shared the story of a new CEO who, from his first meeting with the

CDO, and despite patient and thoughtful feedback suggesting alternatives, maintained that he would meet with potential donors only in his office, and only when they were ready to make a commitment. Naturally, the CDO was asking trusted friends and advisors for advice.

CDOs also need their CEOs to back them up. "When board members lose confidence in a CDO or any senior officer, they usually didn't come to that conclusion all by themselves," says Randy Helm, president of Muhlenberg College. "I try never to vent about frustrations with a cabinet member to trustees unless there is a serious problem that requires board involvement. Senior staff need to know you are holding them accountable for their performance, but also that you have their back when there are unavoidable bumps in the road."

CEO Staff and Executive Assistants

Open and healthy relationships with members of the CEO office staff are also critically important. CEO offices have expanded in recent years: Many now include a chief of staff, an office manager, strategic planning assistants, and board liaisons. Meetings involving these staff members often have implications for development programs, and CDOs can't be present for every discussion. Staff members who know and trust CDOs will exert extra effort to keep them informed.

Wise CDOs are appropriately respectful and friendly toward executive assistants! Executive assistants of CEOs and other senior leaders juggle hundreds of requests, often needing to play the role of gatekeeper. Those who like CDOs are much more inclined to squeeze in a meeting or phone call or get an answer to an urgent question. When five equally important people are waiting for the CEO and hoping to catch five minutes when another meeting ends early, executive assistants usually determine whose message is on top of the pile.

OTHER SENIOR LEADERS

Healthy CDO relationships with board members and with other senior officers fortify the CDO-CEO partnership. Thus, CDOs maintain regular contact with those most closely connected to CEOs: other direct reports of the CEO and board members. Calendars are likely to feature at least one meal each week with a senior colleague and another with a board member, allowing them to build personal as well as professional relationships with the organization's most powerful and influential leaders in a less formal setting.

CDOs also pay careful attention to power brokers beyond board members and members of CEO cabinets. Timothy Higdon, former CDO, consultant, and adjunct assistant professor at New York University's George H. Heyman, Jr., Center for Philanthropy and Fundraising, points out that "the hierarchy on the organization chart as well as the hierarchy of a board can be very different than the reality of who holds the most power. The most effective CDOs read people well and quickly assess how best to navigate within their organizations."

Moreover, top CDOs exercise excellent judgment in the handling of personal and professional tensions that arise between CEOs and other organizational leaders. Inevitably, senior officers and trustees will have differences of opinion with CEOs and may vent frustration to, or in the presence of, CDOs. Even if they agree, CDOs must always remember: *Speak and act at all times as though your CEO is sitting next to you, and you will be much more likely to do the right thing.*

As members of the executive team, CDOs also need to be well aligned with programmatic leaders throughout the organization, such as faculty members, physicians, and artistic leaders. In the words of David Ressler, CEO of the Aspen Valley Hospital, "It is sometimes said that boards hire CEOs and medical staff fire CEOs. A CDO who fails to gain the respect of leading medical staff members can damage the effectiveness of an entire executive team, and ultimately that of a CEO." Jerry May, vice president of development at the University of Michigan, adds, "CDOs who rely too heavily on the confidence of the CEO and don't build bridges to programmatic leaders make a huge, and often costly, mistake."

The Chief Financial Officer

The relationship between CDOs and chief financial officers (CFOs) continues to grow in significance. "The importance of the CDO-CFO relationship has changed dramatically in recent years," says Robbee Kosak, vice president of university advancement at Carnegie Mellon University. "It is at their peril that today's CDOs operate without strong, highly effective relationships with their CFOs." Several leading consultants report that they devote substantial and increasing time to repairing and strengthening CDO-CFO relationships.

"One of the best pieces of advice I ever got was from Wilbur 'Bill' Pierpont, legendary vice president emeritus and professor emeritus of accounting," says Jerry May. "Early in my career, he told me, 'Whatever you do, you are going to have conflicts with your CFO, and you never, ever, want to let your bridge with the CFO be burned.' Strong relationships with CFOs have been among the most important contributors to whatever success I've had in development."

Preparing for CEO Transition

CEO transitions provide opportunities for fundraising connected to the out-going CEO and to the incoming CEO. These are discussed in more detail in chapter 4. Transitions also create uncertainty for CDOs. Given the extreme pressure on CEOs connected with fundraising, new CEOs often want to bring in their own teams.

It is arguably a mistake for a CEO to hire a new CDO without giving an existing CDO a chance, but it is also a mistake to wait too long to make a change when it is necessary. A CDO who has built strong relationships with senior leaders throughout an organization will have many more advocates when a new CEO is measuring that CDO's potential contribution to that CEO's team. But even with many healthy relationships and with strong track records of success, CDOs sometimes find themselves out of work when new CEOs come on board.

Understanding this dynamic, wise CDOs reach out early to newly appointed CEOs. They offer to visit CEOs-elect before they take office, share information about their development programs and especially about potential for growth, and otherwise communicate directly their desire to make new CEOs successful. They also keep their eyes open for other opportunities, should the fit with a new CEO not be a good one.

Balancing Competing Priorities

Given the pressure to raise money, and given the healthy egos required for effective leadership, it is understandable that senior leaders throughout an organization aggressively pursue the strategic objectives most important to them. Sometimes those competing for fundraising revenue want CDOs to negotiate a compromise—in which the CEO might present a donor with multiple options, or with a proposal to support multiple programs. Just as often, they want CDOs to achieve an outcome that meets *their* specific and immediate need, regardless of whether it is the best outcome for the organization as a whole. CDOs must balance these competing needs, align them with organizational priorities, and maintain healthy relationships with all involved parties.

Consider the following scenario, involving a couple with great wealth. They have never made a major gift, and she has just become engaged through her local alumni club. She graduated from the business school, and he is a cardiology patient in the university's medical center:

- The dean: "She is a graduate of my school, and you need to tell the president that I can't get done what I was hired to do if you and he are taking all the best prospects."

- The president: "She is a graduate of the university, and the dean is just going to have to accept that in this case, my priorities come first."
- The hospital CEO: "We need every top prospective donor focused first and foremost on the new children's hospital building, or we'll never reach our goal."
- The chief of cardiology: "I just saved that donor's life! I'm sure my research means more to him than a new children's hospital."
- The campaign chair: "The friends group chair needs to realize that fund-raising is job number 1."
- The friends group chair: "Our job is friend-raising; we need to get these people involved before anyone asks them for money."
- The chief financial officer: "We need unrestricted giving to hit $6 million this year or we won't make budget."
- The trustee development committee chair: "The chief financial officer wants to balance the budget, but if we don't raise another $3 million for the endowment challenge given by my fellow trustee, we'll lose the challenge gift and offend our biggest donor."

Each individual is focused on the area for which he or she has accepted responsibility. Their passion for what they do will sometimes lead to unproductive wrangling, as they compete for a potential donor's attention and philanthropy. Their organizations, however, *count on them* to meet varying objectives.

Rather than taking sides, CDOs inculcate a climate of trust and respect for individual roles that permits the organization to succeed not only in spite of, but *often because of*, this inevitable competition of exciting and inspirational ideas. They build relationships with leaders, among leaders, and between development staff and leaders. By listening to aspirations throughout the organization, they illuminate opportunities for synergy, actively participate in organization-wide priority setting, and help shape fundraising objectives that allow for the realization of the greatest possible number of established priorities.

Of course, not every senior leader will be pleased with every cultivation strategy or every gift solicitation. But, if they believe that their voices are heard, if they participate in discussions and hear other perspectives, and if they have confidence that their CDOs appreciate their responsibilities and are committed to helping them succeed, they will be more likely to support their CDOs when things don't go their way.

Sometimes the best strategy to deal with competing priorities is to turn internal competitors into internal collaborators. A CDO colleague once worked with two deans who had done a wonderful job, separately, of cultivating a very generous couple. The couple had degrees from both schools. The deans had a great relationship with each other, but they each privately made clear to the CDO that the couple could be asked for only one gift, and "it had better not be for that other dean's school."

Rather than ignoring one dean or trying to negotiate with both deans—perhaps working out a "deal" that might make no sense at all to the donors—the CDO suggested the deans meet with the donors together. The result was a joint gift and, importantly, the donors remarked that they were pleased to see how collaborative the two deans were and that this added tremendously to their *confidence* in making the gift. Equally important, the creative solution proposed by the CDO resulted in strengthened relationships when the conflict could easily have damaged them.

Building Consensus around Established Priorities

Choosing top priorities for the organization among competing priorities across the organization means making difficult choices. CEOs sometimes hesitate to make choices that could alienate other senior leaders within the organization. Effective CDOs help their CEOs by facilitating participation and communication among all constituents throughout the priority-setting process, and by gently but persistently seeking resolution and clarity around priorities. They then play a critical role in building the widest possible consensus around priorities.

The best laid plans of CEO, CDO, and board chairman can fall apart, for example, when an organizational leader and friend of the prospective donor is unaware of, or possibly even opposed to, the giving opportunity presented as a leading organizational priority. The larger the gift under discussion, the greater the likelihood will be that the prospective donor has many relationships across the organization, increasing the possibility that gift conversations will derail.

It is therefore critical that CDOs ensure that the fundraising priorities of the organization are clearly articulated, well understood, and widely endorsed across the leadership of the organization. Donors with significant capacity are pursued relentlessly and by innumerable organizations. Solicitors try to separate their organizations from all others by creating giving opportunities that donors will find "too good to pass up." Donors sort through all the glossy brochures with fancy words and lofty promises to find opportunities to make gifts that will have major impact on the organization— gifts that will "work" because the organization is *fully behind the project*. Prospective donors will have confidence that their proposed gifts are a wise investment when they hear a consistent story.

Creating Understanding of How Development Works

CDOs, by regularly taking part in the events of other departments within their organizations, bolster support for the development office. Their participation builds credibility among colleagues in all parts of the organization, and it simultaneously enhances the development staff's understanding and support of their colleagues' responsibilities and priorities. As Dexter Bailey, vice president for university advancement at Stony Brook University, reminds us, "Most of our colleagues in other parts of the organization and outside the organization still don't understand what development officers do." A provost of another institution put it this way, only half joking: "For development staff, every day is a party."

By attending meetings, classes, lectures, and performances, CDOs demonstrate their interest in the work of colleagues, and the interactions give their colleagues the chance to get to know them and understand their work. In addition, this support creates goodwill: A professional orchestra musician, asked by the development office to perform for an event or attend a house party, is much more willing to agree if she has noticed that orchestra's CDO attending concerts on a regular basis.

Having the trust and understanding of senior leadership makes it much easier to secure additional resources for the development program when they are needed. "CDOs without sufficient resources to hire and support excellent staff members are bound to fail," says Jerry May. "The only way to win the resources required for a successful program is to develop and sustain a high level of credibility with organizational leaders. Developing this credibility must be among the highest priorities for new CDOs."

Relationships with Senior Leaders beyond the Organization

In a recent Council for Advancement and Support of Education conference on the subject of what the future holds for CDOs, Darrow Zeidenstein, Senior Vice President at Rice University, suggested that collaboration and consolidation—within large organizations, among organizations within a community, and among organizations with related missions—was increasing and likely to accelerate in rate of increase. Effective CDOs explore and promote opportunities for collaboration and support their CEOs in doing so, and they respond to increased complexity with flexibility and creativity.

Donors often support organizations with complementary missions as well as organizations with overlapping missions. They want all to succeed, but not one at the expense of another, and they appreciate when synergy results in greater efficiency and impact of each philanthropic dollar.

The largest gift ever received by National Public Radio came from Joan Kroc, a longtime supporter of her local public radio station in San Diego. As

Mrs. Kroc neared the end of her life, Stephanie Bergsma, the CDO at San Diego's KPBS, reached out to Kevin Klose, the president of NPR. Aware of Mrs. Kroc's love of public broadcasting and her significant giving capacity, Stephanie worked with NPR to present the case for a transformational gift. Focusing on the donor and on public radio more broadly, she also emphasized the compatibility of, rather than differences between, two separate nonprofits (KPBS and NPR), and her collaborative approach led to a gift of more than $200 million to NPR as well as the largest gift ever received by KPBS.

Similarly, when Alan Fletcher became president and CEO of the Aspen Music Festival and School, he learned that Jazz Aspen Snowmass, a separate organization with a complementary mission, was spending enormous amounts of money each summer to erect a temporary tent for its jazz festival. Alan arranged to rent his organization's permanent tent structure to Jazz Aspen, and hundreds in the donor community were thrilled, grateful that fewer of their philanthropic dollars would be spent on facility requirements and more could go directly to programming. The benefit went both ways; dozens of Jazz patrons came to the Music Festival tent for the first time.

In another example, the Aspen Santa Fe Ballet, whose mission also overlaps with that of the Music Festival, had never performed in the Music Festival's tent—a venue that seats 2,000—and had never performed with a live orchestra. A few individuals opposed to the collaboration argued that the Ballet would steal the Music Festival's donors. Instead, ballet dancers had the opportunity to perform with live music, students in the Aspen Music Festival and School program had the opportunity to learn and perform ballet music, audiences enjoyed performances they otherwise would not have seen in Aspen, and board members and other donors saw their investments extending the fulfillment of the missions of both organizations.

CDOs who develop and support effective relationships with leaders of complementary organizations in their community create opportunity and strengthen philanthropy. Their organizations find ways to fulfill their missions more effectively or more efficiently through collaboration than in isolation. Organizations win, donors win, and communities win.

TOP DONORS AND VOLUNTEERS

CDOs hold primary responsibility for the stewardship of their organizations' relationships with all top donors and volunteers. Their organizations count on them to

- maintain up-to-date, accurate biographical information;

- record information related to cultivation, solicitation, and stewardship activity;
- ensure that all gifts are properly recorded, receipted, and acknowledged in a timely manner;
- keep track of each donor's and each volunteer's connections with the organization;
- create communications, events, and other activities designed to initiate and strengthen relationships; and
- engage organizational leaders and other appropriate individuals in building and sustaining relationships.

Organizations also expect CDOs to play one of the principal roles in face-to-face contact with donors, prospective donors, and volunteers, especially board members and top donors. Personal relationships forged by CDOs augment those of CEOs, board chairs, and other senior leaders. CDOs with strong donor relationships are better prepared to advise senior colleagues involved in the cultivation and solicitation of those donors. CDOs are prepared to play a supporting role when CEOs or others have the lead role in a solicitation, share the lead role in a solicitation, or take the lead as needed.

CDOs facilitate effective relationships between other organizational leaders and top donors and volunteers, promote mutually reinforcing relationships between and among top donors and volunteers, and oversee staff members responsible for building these relationships. They support and strengthen these relationships by building a culture that views donors and volunteers as "insiders"—partners in creating the future of the organizations they support. Chapter 2 discusses in detail the shaping of such a culture.

Friendships Sometimes Evolve, but Remember the Primary Reason for the Relationship

CDOs have access to powerful, influential people, but they are not usually in the same social circles. The reason they have access is their professional position, not their social position. Thus, while friendships sometimes naturally develop, CDOs who strive for these friendships, forgetting the main reasons for their interaction, are usually disappointed. Exceptions do exist: "While it is not a fundraiser's mission to become personal friends with donors, if, over time, friendships with them evolve, it would be wrong to dismiss them," says David Dunlop, founding director of the principal gifts program at Cornell University.

RELATIONSHIPS WITH #2s

CDOs make relationships with their most senior direct reports a high priority. The success of CDOs depends upon the success of their direct reports. These individuals handle the day-to-day management of the department, and some of them will succeed their CDOs or move into CDO roles in other organizations. They need access to the CDO and to other senior leaders, provided by the CDO, in order to be successful. During a CDO transition, CEOs rely on strong and well-prepared #2s for stability and continuity.

David Unruh served as associate vice president for development at the University of Chicago during my tenure as vice president. David and I met almost every Tuesday evening over dinner—sometimes for two hours, most times for four or five hours. After discussing weekly agenda items, we would talk at length about larger issues, such as organizational politics, major concerns of the president and board leadership, strategic and financial planning, and governance challenges. These meetings provided a safe and secure environment in which to deal with complex and frustrating issues and simultaneously gave David insights he would need as a CDO (after our work together in Chicago, David accepted his first CDO role, as senior vice president at Temple University).

"Given the demands on CDOs from many directions, a strong #2 is more important than ever," says David Unruh. "Without a strong #2, CDOs don't have the flexibility they need for full-fledged partnership with the president, board, and other senior officers."

THE DEVELOPMENT STAFF

Successful CDOs excel at identifying, hiring, and retaining talented and promising development professionals and at creating relationships that last a lifetime. They hire and appoint managers who know how to build strong relationships with donors *and* with colleagues and staff members. They engender a culture that fosters healthy relationships across departmental and divisional boundaries. This is discussed further in chapter 8.

During my tenure, the University of Chicago alumni relations and development staff spent a year creating a mission statement, vision statement, and values statement for the division. The values statement reads, "The University of Chicago exists 'to grow knowledge so that human life may be enriched.' Our volunteers and donors are essential partners in furthering this mission. In working with them to secure support for that mission, we aspire to a level of excellence that complements that which is expected of and by our faculty, students, alumni, and other members of our University of Chicago community. *Since our success is defined by the generosity of others, we in turn are generous with each other, investing in and celebrating the success of the work we do together."*

Relationships within the Department

In small shops, staff members by necessity wear many hats. As the size of the development shop increases, however, job descriptions of staff members tend to become more specialized. Relationships among staff members as well as with donors become harder to build and sustain. In large shops, staff members may focus on a specific type of fundraising such as annual giving, planned or deferred giving, major gifts, or corporate and foundation giving; on an operational unit of the organization such as a cancer department, library, or law school; on a constituency such as subscribers, parents, patients, or fraternity/sorority alumni; or on a geographical region such as Greater New York City, the U.S. West Coast, or Asia.

This division of focus may improve efficiency and permit the organization to support a larger number and variety of constituents, but it also creates tremendous potential for rivalry that can damage staff relationships and donor relationships. The most successful development programs are those in which CDOs encourage staff members to view colleagues not as competitors, but rather as individuals with diverse perspectives and areas of expertise essential for the success of the team as a whole.

No one "owns" a prospect—that kind of thinking has no place in fundraising. Rather, to develop the strongest possible bond between donor and organization, enlightened development officers talk to staff colleagues to attain a comprehensive view of donor interests and status. In creating a strategy for a new prospective donor, they might, for example, enlist the help of their various colleagues who

- work in the prospective donor's region;
- work with other donors who are friends of the prospective donor;
- work with the department the prospective donor is interested in supporting; and
- work on the type of gift the prospective donor is considering.

The pressures of goals and deadlines work against this level of collaboration, but a commitment to this approach creates a better team, stronger relationships, and better results. CDOs reinforce this approach through highlighting successful collaborative efforts, and through hiring and promoting staff members and managers with shared values.

Metrics

A great deal of emphasis has been placed on metrics in recent years. Proponents argue that increased measurement of return on investments made in the fundraising program, and of productivity of frontline development staff, for example, will lead to greater efficiency and effectiveness of fundraising efforts. Without any doubt, some measurement is important. But inappropriate use of metrics in fundraising presents a pitfall to the relationship builder in chief.

Even the most philanthropic people rarely have giving at the top of their mind. Donors need to be invited and encouraged to give, they need to be thanked, and they need to be told about the impact their gifts have had on the organization. Measuring interaction with and engagement of donors and prospective donors is certainly important. The quality of engagement, however, is at least as important as the quantity, though it is much harder to measure. Measuring quantity only can inadvertently incentivize behaviors, such as ill-timed visits or gift solicitations, that are counterproductive to the building of healthy, long-term relationships with donors.

Fundraising progress, in total number of donors, total number of gifts, and total amount of giving, for example, must also be measured. Evaluating the productivity of frontline development officers based on the amount of money given by "their" donors, however, is problematic, in that credit for the gift in a collaborative environment often belongs to others in addition to the gift officer, and on occasion to someone else altogether. Individual "credit" usually works against the promotion of the type of relationships that are the hallmark of a healthy team.

The Lone Ranger

Successful CDOs know that lone rangers destroy teams and that a good development officer is more a "liaison" or "facilitator" than a "rainmaker." A candidate whose resume includes a claim of millions of dollars personally raised is suspect; no one is solely responsible for the generous act of a donor. Many CDOs won't even bother meeting with a candidate whose resume contains such a claim.

In celebrating gifts, CDOs recognize the efforts of an array of people, including, for example, the prospect researcher who first identified but has never met the donor, or the donor's friend who first introduced the donor to the organization. The seed of a gift secured today was likely planted years ago and nurtured by countless individuals whose roles in the cultivation of the gift will never be known. Furthermore, successful CDOs regularly and visibly celebrate gifts not only as achievements of the development office and development volunteers, but also—and most importantly—as expressions of belief in the organization's mission and confidence in its future. They expect their staff members to do the same.

THE LARGER COMMUNITY

"Strengthening relations in the community, learning from one's neighbors, taking the time to meet and greet fellow citizens will not only yield forms of support, it will engender goodwill and positive feeling," says Reynold Levy, president of Lincoln Center for the Performing Arts. "In the ATM machine of life, such visits will create deposits of high value. Rest assured, the time will come when withdrawals are needed."[1] CDOs pay attention to the organization's community, including neighbors, local business leaders, local legislators, and local nonprofit leaders. They build relationships with some, and they encourage and support additional relationships involving their colleagues.

SUMMARY

Excellence in relationship building with *donors* is essential for all frontline *fundraisers*. To be successful today, however, **CDOs** must do much more, building and sustaining strong relationships with and among *all internal and external constituents* of their organizations.

PREPARING FOR THE ROLE

"Before I was in the top role, there were people I didn't get along with especially well, and I could still succeed," said one CDO. "In the top job, I feel I won't succeed if I can't navigate all of my relationships; any of them could be my undoing. I might not lose my job, but I won't reach my potential as CDO. It's imperative that I cultivate positive relationships that allow me to work across functions, across teams, and across the whole organizational community. I had to start really good at it, and I have to get better every day."

Expect the Best

In *Designs for Fund-Raising,* still one of the most important books for a fundraising leader, Harold "Si" Seymour writes, "I would beg you to believe—as I do now and always have—that most of the people are very wonderful indeed, that they almost always wish to do the right thing, and that their ultimate performance, when boldly challenged and confidently led, is usually far better than we have any right to expect. Study them and treat them well, for you need them more than money."[2]

Successful development officers look for and expect the best in others. They are quick to celebrate others' success and slow to criticize. They discourage negativity, and they remind colleagues that donors do not "owe" gifts to anyone. Each gift, no matter the size, is a cause for celebration. "Everyone has an angel on one shoulder, and a devil on the other," says Jim Thompson, senior vice president and chief advancement officer at the University of Rochester. "We appeal to the angels and help them grow."

Cultivate Olympic-Level Relationship-Building Skills

Early in their careers, usually as frontline development officers, aspiring CDOs learn how to listen with great care to the wishes, hopes, dreams, and concerns of potential donors and their families and how to bring an organization's needs and donor objectives into productive alignment. "Successful development officers can put themselves in the shoes of donors," says Elizabeth Boluch Wood, vice president for development at Princeton University. "They will draw heavily on that skill as CDOs, when they will need to be able to put themselves in the shoes of a wide variety of institutional leaders to understand the leaders' perspectives and priorities."

In early management roles, such as director of major gifts, aspiring CDOs widen their circle of relationships to include more staff colleagues as well as development professionals outside their organizations. They also learn the importance of rising above rather than feeding into personal and professional clashes, especially among staff members.

Newly appointed CDOs ideally bring to their roles excellent relationship-building skills forged in previous frontline fundraising and management positions. They go on to expand their skills. Susan Washburn gives an example: "The development officer builds listening skills into active listening skills, and the CDO has to expand active listening skills into *Olympic* listening skills." In preparing for the role, practice, practice, practice.

Handle Difficult Situations in Person

When the potential for misunderstanding or disagreement arises, rather than firing off a quick e-mail, pick up the phone, or even better, go in person. Two of my closest personal friendships are with deans who had had some tense interactions with university administration, including development, due to the natural competition over donors between schools and the university as a whole.

Despite staff colleagues telling me not to "waste my time," I invested many hours in building these relationships. This included face-to-face meetings whenever I had something substantive to discuss. Even when a phone call or e-mail might have sufficed, I chose to go to the dean's office in person, much as I would do with a trustee or major donor. With each dean— one at Carnegie Mellon University, and the other at the University of Chicago—I had the opportunity to collaborate on the largest gift that university had ever received ($55 million, and $300 million, respectively). In both cases, we established what have become lifelong friendships.

Lower the Temperature

Instead of responding to *disagreements between colleagues* in a way that raises the temperature, endeavor to understand the perspectives and passion that create disagreements and focus your energy on leading colleagues through and past conflict. Jim Thompson refers to this role as that of Chief Interpreting Officer. He often reminds his staff, "Seek first to understand." Those who will succeed in the role of CDO give colleagues the benefit of the doubt until all facts and motivations are understood, and they deal with disagreements privately, avoiding embarrassment of colleagues and the potential for lasting bad feelings.

Similarly, instead of responding to a *situation* in a way that raises the temperature, get the facts and communicate openly. In the mid-2000s, the CDO at a leading university was involved with the president and other senior officers in handling several situations that caused tensions on campus and significant press coverage around Middle Eastern politics. She and her colleagues developed talking points and encouraged fundraising staff to speak proactively and directly with concerned donors, thus reducing the volatility of the situation.

Successful development officers excel at injecting energy and passion, raising sights, enhancing belief and confidence, and creating excitement. However, "CDOs are calm in periods of crisis," says Elizabeth Boluch Wood. "The last thing you need is any susceptibility to panic." Those preparing to be CDOs need to learn to defuse tension and restore calm in the midst of situations with potential to damage relationships important to the health of the team and the organization.

ADDITIONAL WAYS TO PREPARE

- Don't shy away from difficult donors, difficult colleagues, or difficult situations. Volunteer to work with them, and learn from them. As CDO, you will personally encounter many difficult individuals and situations and will be called upon to advise the CEO in others. The more practice you have, the more often you will succeed at handling them successfully.

- Get to know your organization's power brokers, the key administrative, programmatic, and volunteer leaders. Be a collaborative team player and demonstrate that you respect their roles and contributions. You will spend as much or more time building relationships with these individuals as with donors and therefore need to learn early on how to identify and cultivate excellent relationships with them.
- Get to know colleagues in other departments and learn about how a non-profit organization works. Many CDOs interviewed had worked for some period in a nonprofit field other than development, such as marketing, admissions, or finance. They cited an understanding of the roles of other nonprofit divisions as a great benefit.
- Volunteer for special task forces and committees that give you the opportunity to build relationships with colleagues outside of your normal circle.
- Serve on your own alumni association as a volunteer.
- Welcome people who challenge your assumptions, and allow them to correct your mistakes and sharpen your arguments.
- Study and practice the art of negotiation.
- Steward your entire team as carefully as you steward donors. Happy and fulfilled employees do a better job, they build healthier relationships with donors, and they stay. Work hard to keep star employees, yet don't be afraid to cut underperformers. Resolve problems creatively, through continuing education, schedule flexibility, and many other benefits; they are much less expensive than toxic morale and a revolving door. Learn to position yourself and your team in the context of a larger framework.
- Learn to manage up, across, and down at the same time, juggling and prioritizing the needs of different groups.
- Identify CDO role models who manage difficult situations and relationships well. Study them, and emulate styles and methods that feel right to you.
- Speak with other senior officers (chief financial officer, chief marketing and communications officer, etc.); ask about the challenges they face and how they think CDOs can help them.
- Create a group of those individuals within your organization or broader community who have similar aspirations, and meet with them regularly to exchange ideas. Invite more-experienced CDOs or senior officers to attend as guest speakers.
- Become known for excellence in customer service. Return calls within 24 hours, if not sooner. Learn to be a great listener and create customer-oriented teams among staff and colleagues.
- Finally, when you interview for a CDO position, be sure that you are a wonderful fit with the CEO. This partnership is critical to success.

NOTES

1. Reynold Levy, *Yours for the Asking* (Wiley, 2009), 80.
2. Harold Seymour, *Designs for Fund-Raising* (McGraw-Hill, 1966), 16.

Chapter Two

Shaper of Culture That Embraces Philanthropic Partnership

Successful CDOs shape and consistently reinforce a culture in which donors are viewed, throughout the organization, as partners in the fulfillment of mission. Knowing that donors and prospective donors who are well-informed, interested, involved, and invested in the future of an organization are much more likely to give repeatedly and generously, they eliminate language and activity that would distance donors, promoting instead language and activity that underscore the donors' essential role in creating the past, present, and future of our nation's nonprofit organizations. In other words, donors are treated as insiders rather than outsiders. As a result, donors and organizational leaders speak of each other and the organization in the first person: "*We* save lives." "*We* provide a world-class education." "*Our* goal is to bring the arts to every child in the region."

For generations, generous individuals and families have built our nation's great institutions, from schools to museums, and from hospitals to concert halls. They feel a well-deserved sense of pride and ownership in them. Most of an organization's top donors have given over years, if not decades, and usually over a longer period than any development officer, CEO, or board member has been on the scene. In the words of Si Seymour, "There can hardly be any stronger motivation for supporting a group or cause than simple pride of association."[1]

CDOs also instill a culture of ownership of fundraising efforts within the organization. "More than fundraising, our roles involve institutionalizing advancement," says Connie Kravas, vice president for university advancement and president of the University of Washington Foundation. "We serve and support all the organization's leaders; advancement is successful when it becomes *their* program."

CDOs frame organization-wide conversations that focus on what might be accomplished rather than what might be raised. This focus invites donors into a philanthropic partnership, where their values and objectives are as important as those of the organizations they support. When the focus is on what's possible, rather than on need, even organizations perceived to be very wealthy are still enormously successful in raising money.

At the same time, effective CDOs never lose sight of their organizations' missions. "If you change who you are simply to raise money, you've lost everything, and you've sold out," says David Ressler. "We need to understand what excites our donors, educate donors about our mission, and pull the two together. The real art is in shaping gifts that incorporate the best thinking from our donors and simultaneously advance our ability to fulfill our core mission."

"A PARTNERSHIP DISTRIBUTION"

In announcing his family's gift of $300 million to the University of Chicago in 2008, David Booth said, "It's not a gift. The university has been a partner all along, so this is a partnership distribution."[2] Many people played a role in cultivating and soliciting that gift, beginning with David's professors. Deans, presidents, fellow board members, development staff members, and alumni reinforced the donor's sense of partnership over many years.

"I WANTED TO BE A PART OF IT"

When David Tepper announced his gift of $55 million to Carnegie Mellon University in 2004, he said, "To come from Peabody High School and be able to do this in my life is just amazing. . . . Dean Dunn is making some fantastic and strategic changes to the school's curriculum and focus. He needs resources, and I wanted to be a part of it."[3] The donor did not consider his gift a transfer of money from his family to an organization but, rather, a partnership investment in the future of a school that now bears his name.

"WE ARE DEEPLY GRATEFUL FOR THEIR VISION AND PARTNERSHIP"

"A gift of such magnitude will impact not only the festival, but the entire classical music world as it will catapult this institution to a new level of excellence and international influence," said Alan Fletcher, president and CEO of the Aspen Music Festival and School (AMFS), announcing a gift of $25 million from Matthew and Kay Bucksbaum, the largest gift in the institution's history. "We are deeply grateful for their vision and partnership."[4]

"The festival is a truly special place," Matthew Bucksbaum says. "Kay and I have long believed in it, especially the incredible students whose energy keeps classical music vital."[5] Matthew served two terms, and Kay one term, as board chair of the AMFS. Their objective was keeping classical music vital, and their partner in doing so was the music festival and school they had known and loved for more than 50 years.

MANY POINTS OF CONNECTION ARE BETTER THAN ONE

Successful CDOs engage organizational leaders, including board members and other top donors, in building multiple—often dozens of—relationships with donors and prospective donors. More relationships lead to more frequent contact, more opportunities for involvement, a more comprehensive perspective for the donor, and better information on the donor for the organization. Connections for both donor and organization become more personal and enduring.

While key decision makers, such as administrative and board leaders, give donors confidence that the organizations in which they are investing are well managed, interactions with others within the organization enhance a donor's feeling of connection. The more involved and invested the donor, the more these relationships should be encouraged and supported. Any individual who shares a donor's passion has the potential to reinforce that donor's commitment to the organization. In fact, faculty members, students, physicians, researchers, curators, or orchestra musicians are often the best people to inspire a gift, bringing the elements of a proposal to life.

Multiple points of connection ensure the continuity of the partnership between donor and organization. Administrative leaders often change jobs, retire, or leave the organization. Volunteer leaders may shift leadership positions or take breaks between periods of service. These individual transitions cause little or no disruption in the philanthropy of donors who have strong relationships with many throughout the organization.

DONOR AND ORGANIZATIONAL
GOALS ARE *BOTH* IMPORTANT

Leaders are under tremendous pressure to achieve organizational goals. In this context, they can lose sight of, or even become annoyed by, donor objectives when they do not directly align with those of the organization. They may come to feel that donors are distracting them from agreed-upon priorities. Furthermore, donors do not organize their lives around the fiscal years or campaign timelines of organizations and are often unaware of them. Successful CDOs help organizational leaders and donors find common

ground, understanding that fundraising done right is generally better than
fundraising done quickly.

GRATITUDE FOR EVERY GIFT

Some organizational leaders, particularly those who are highly accomplished
but without great personal wealth, resent those born with wealth and those
who have accumulated hundreds of millions or billions of dollars in a short
period of time. Rarely is such resentment overtly expressed, but it may
underlie such statements as, "I can't believe he turned us down; he wouldn't
even miss that $10 million." CDOs remind everyone that no gift is "owed"
and every gift warrants only gratitude. Robert Sharpe, president of the Sharpe
Group, puts it this way: "When asking becomes *demanding*, then giving can
become *taking*."

CHANGING THE WORLD

Above all, philanthropic partners want to get something done. "For your
prospects, giving is about changing lives and saving lives. It's not about the
money," says Jerold Panas.[6] During my tenure at Carnegie Mellon University, when Ken Dunn began his conversation with donor David Tepper, we
hoped that David would become excited enough about Ken's and the
school's vision to make a major gift. We had no idea David would go on to
make the largest gift, at the time, in Carnegie Mellon's history. Rather than
asking for a gift, Ken described his dream and then paused. In David's
response, Ken understood that he had found a partner, and that David's
principal concern would be making sure the dream could come to fruition.

LEVERAGING EACH OTHER'S ASSETS

Asking potential donors to partner with an organization is much easier than
asking them for money. We spend our lives figuring out how to provide for
ourselves and for our families. In a sense, then, giving away money is unnat-
ural, and asking someone else to give away money is uncomfortable. Asking
someone to cooperate for *mutual* benefit is, for most, a much less awkward
proposition.

In philanthropic partnerships, donors come to the table with ideas and
with financial resources. Organizations come to the table with ideas and with
mission, expertise, infrastructure, reputation, endowment, gifts from others,
and a host of other resources. Through partnership, *donors accomplish something they could not do without the organization, and organizations accomplish something they could not do without the donor*. Understanding this

fully, CDOs prepare their organizations' leaders to come to the table as potential partners, rather than supplicants, prepared to ask with confidence.

In announcing a $150 million gift from Dorothy and Robert King to establish the Stanford Institute for Innovation in Developing Economies, Stanford University President John Hennessy said, "With tremendous fore-sight and compassion, the Kings have made a seminal gift that leverages Stanford's knowledge, resources, and human capital to make a real differ-ence in the world for many years to come."[7] In speaking about the same gift, Mrs. King said, "The relationships the university has in Silicon Valley, the range of expertise it has among its professors—it can't be replicated. The university can make our money more fruitful than we could on our own."[8] This gift and the words of university president and donor clearly illustrate the concept of philanthropic partnership: organization and donor leveraging each other's assets to accomplish something extraordinary.

PHILANTHROPIC PARTNERSHIPS AREN'T BUILT IN A DAY

Philanthropic partnerships develop over time. In the beginning, new donors with good intentions may have ideas not well aligned with organizational priorities. Their ideas may be ones long ago rejected by the organization, or ones the organization would and should never even consider. These donors do not yet know the institution. CDOs help administrative and volunteer leaders demonstrate patience with new potential philanthropic partners, rec-ognizing that outright rejection of their ideas can lead to long-term if not permanent loss of potential donor relationships.

Similarly, organizational leaders and fundraisers can stumble with new donors by coming to them with well-developed plans and expecting to win their support, often spending hours plotting out scenario after scenario and crafting answers to every possible question and objection, but failing to recognize the importance of letting the donors inform the plans as they are being developed.

Jerold Panas quotes a donor, Homer Watkins: "They come marching in here with their ideas and their fancy proposals. They don't ask what I'm interested in. They're only concerned with telling me what they want me to buy. It is impossible for me to get involved in that kind of a situation." Panas adds his own comment: "As Watkins makes clear, too often in fundraising the programs that might be the most important to your organization are irrelevant to the major donor."[9]

Top CDOs invest the time necessary to bring goals and objectives of the donor and those of the organization into alignment. As existing and potential donors become more involved, they learn about and even help shape strategic objectives, and *organizational* objectives begin to become *their* objectives.

Major gifts sometimes require no "ask" at all. When potential donors embrace an organization's strategic objectives as their own, gifts may be entirely self-solicited, and multiple gifts more readily occur, as donors ensure that objectives they have adopted materialize. When leaders start with this end in mind, they build relationships that last.

DONORS HAVE GOOD IDEAS

Donors, if given the opportunity, will often improve organizations' plans. "Existing and potential donors are frequently sources of excellent advice and guidance. Many rich people achieve their success by keeping well informed and alert; by being curious and by asking probing, even impertinent questions," says Reynold Levy.[10] In addition to improving the chances of alignment between donor and organizational objectives, openness to donor input often leads to better ideas and sharpens cases for support, increasing their appeal to other donors.

DONORS INSPIRE OTHER DONORS

Donors are essential partners in fundraising efforts with other donors. "When staff members are the only voices involved in asking, it is a sign of an impoverished development program," says David Dunlop. "Donors add the voice of those who have done themselves what others are being asked to do, at whatever exemplary level that might be. Involving them not only increases the effectiveness of requests; it also recognizes their uniqueness as members of a very special group of organizational friends."

DONOR INTERESTS CHANGE OVER TIME

It is easy to assume that earlier associations, such as the program or school attended, will accurately reflect the current interests of a donor. Looking backward, organizations may jump to the conclusion that, for instance, a business school graduate would be likely to support a new program in entrepreneurship, while a fine arts alumna would be interested in funding an art history professorship.

Classifying prospective donors based on information that is five, ten, or fifty years old, without taking the time to get to know them and their current wishes for the organization, is typically a mistake. The former business school student may have a great passion for art history. The fine arts graduate may have made her money founding a successful technical startup focused on computer-generated imagery and be much more inspired by the program in entrepreneurship. Often, large organizations offer a breadth of giving opportunities, and top CDOs make connections between today's organization needs and *current* philanthropic objectives of prospective donors.

A leading donor and campaign committee member at Carnegie Mellon, sitting through a campaign planning discussion in which we were reviewing the giving history of our most generous donors, exclaimed, "A donor to this university can satisfy so many philanthropic objectives all in one place! Once they see that we are good stewards of their money, they can have an impact on education, on music, and on cancer research all through gifts to a place they know and trust."

This breadth of giving opportunities does not exist in every nonprofit institution, but each nonprofit institution has the potential to build a multidimensional relationship with its donors. Organizations that see potential donors through a narrow scope inevitably leave money on the table. Organizations that connect with donors and their families on multiple levels receive a greater share of those donors' overall philanthropy, as each gift broadens and deepens the overall donor-organization partnership.

AFFILIATION IS NOT A PREREQUISITE OR EVEN A REQUIREMENT FOR PARTNERSHIP

In May of 1889, John D. Rockefeller pledged a matching grant of $600,000 to establish what became the University of Chicago. His pledge was contingent upon the Chicago Baptists raising an additional $400,000 within one year. The match was met, with most of the gifts below $500, and a large number between $1 and $25.[11] One of the great examples of partnership in philanthropy, Rockefeller's "challenge" gift led to an extraordinary level of civic support of the university from nonalumni Chicagoans—support that continues to this day.

When Robert Hurst became board chair of the Aspen Music Festival and School, he reached out to friends and colleagues who owned homes in Aspen but were not regular concert patrons. He asked them to support the music festival, whether they liked classical music or not, arguing that the music festival was an essential contributor to the health of the community. His appeal resulted in $200,000 in new gifts in the first year.

SUCCESS BREEDS SUCCESS

Organizations that raise large gifts tend to raise *more* large gifts. Multiple donors at the same level give each other added confidence that their gifts are wise investments. Donors join winning teams. Our nation's most successful fundraising organizations continue to raise large gifts not primarily because they *have* needs, but rather because they have a proven track record of partnering with major philanthropists to *meet* needs. CDOs ensure that large gifts are publicized, knowing that successful donor-organization partnerships attract other donors who want their own philanthropic endeavors to succeed.

ORGANIZE FOR SUCCESS

Successful CDOs create a culture that supports a partnership approach among staff. They ensure that

- goals for individual gift officers, departments, and development as a whole incentivize staff to listen carefully to prospective donors, even though gifts might not be credited in the staff member's department or division;
- compensation incentives such as raises and bonuses are tied to the best outcome for donor and organization; and
- management structures, managers, and communications across the organization support behavior that produces the best philanthropic outcomes for the organization as a whole.

GATHER, RECORD, AND USE RELEVANT INFORMATION

CDOs ensure that relationship information is tracked and kept up to date. Databases are filled with information on donors and prospective donors. Gift information is usually the most complete, followed by biographical information, followed distantly by information on donor objectives, wishes, hopes, and dreams. The latter is the most difficult to acquire, but it is the most important. Without it, development officers risk falling into the trap of seeing donors one-dimensionally, with information such as designation of last gift or undergraduate major dictating cultivation and solicitation strategy.

CDOs and consultants share story after story underscoring the same problem: Too much time is spent in the office developing strategies based on scant information instead of visiting face-to-face with donors and asking them about what they hope to accomplish. Even when information is learned directly from donors, it is frequently not captured in a way that will be helpful to future users of the database. To combat this, CDOs ensure that development staff members focus on database fields that matter most: the ones that describe donor intent.

Most disagreements regarding cultivation and solicitation strategy can be resolved when the perspective of the donor is known. When arguments arise in prospect management meetings about the best next steps with a donor, the staff member who has spoken with the donor and can report on the donor's wishes usually, and appropriately, has the most influence on the outcome of the meeting.

PAY ATTENTION TO CONSISTENT DONORS

At the University of Chicago, we studied the giving of the university's donors who had given $10 million or more over their lifetimes. The average span of giving was 33.5 years, the average number of years in which the donors had made gifts was 30, and 71 percent of them supported multiple parts of the university. These donors didn't work with one president; they worked with several. They didn't work with one development officer; they worked with many.

Though some became top donors through one gift, the majority gave many gifts over many years, and they had relationships with dozens, if not hundreds, of administrative leaders, staff members, faculty members, trustees, and many others. Members of every constituency of the University of Chicago touched these donors, and far from damaging the relationship through diversity of perspective, they established bonds so numerous that no individual's departure could sever the philanthropic partnership.

"Many large estate gifts, even those of $1 million or more, come from donors who give small amounts during their lifetimes, in many cases $100 or less per year," says Robert Sharpe. "The consistency and longevity of their giving, much more than the size of annual gifts or the total amount of their giving, predicts the likelihood of a major estate gift. When donors make major estate provisions, they are elevating beneficiary organizations to the status of family member; they don't typically do this unless they've had a long-term giving relationship."

KNOW THE DONOR'S OBJECTIVES

All development officers have had the experience of sitting through prospect strategy sessions, listening to varying and competing opinions on cultivation and solicitation strategies, only to realize that one very important voice is missing: that of the donor. While it is true that part of a development officer's job is to educate prospective donors about institutional priorities, develop new areas of interest, and raise sights, development officers too often fail to start from a place of real understanding of the donors'—and their families'—philanthropic objectives. Effective CDOs ensure that all cultivation and solicitation strategies are informed, as much as possible, by the values and objectives of the relevant donor or prospective donor.

WHEN IN DOUBT, ASK THE DONOR

As simple as it sounds, sometimes the best way to improve CEOs' and other organizational leaders' understanding of donor objectives, and minimize misunderstanding or conflict, is to bring the donor into the conversation. Knowledge of donor objectives among all relevant leaders reduces the potential for internal jealousy or strife among those whose programs don't benefit from that donor's gift. This knowledge will always improve cultivation and solicitation discussions, leading to gifts that are larger and more likely to produce results that make both organization and donor happy. In short, when major institutional leaders who have relationships with donors are bickering over whose program the donor "should" be asked to support, *ask the donor!*

"In preparing for our last campaign, one couple, because of their history of support, appeared on the prospective donor lists of seven different areas of the university," says Connie Kravas. "Clearly, this worried us! We wanted to be respectful of these incredibly philanthropic donors, so we went to them, at the outset, not to ask for a gift, but to seek their guidance.

"We were open and honest," she continues. " 'Because of your history of generosity, it may not surprise you that there are many areas of the university that view you as their closest friends and donors,' we told them. 'We are not here to ask for a gift, but rather to ask for your counsel. Should you choose to make additional contributions during the campaign ahead, we want it to be a truly magnificent experience for you.' Then we listened.

"The couple found the honesty of this approach both appealing and authentic. It led to a clear statement of what they wanted to support and when and how each of the seven programs should approach them. Rather than having a negative reaction to competition among different parts of the university, they felt totally in control. They relished the feeling of being treated as thoughtful partners. That experience was so enlightening that we now ask many of our most generous donors, 'When's the right time to ask? What's the right ask?' "

SUMMARY

Successful *fundraisers* incorporate donor-centered thinking and behavior in their work with *donors and volunteers*. **CDOs** create and sustain *organization-wide* appreciation for the role of philanthropy in the organization's past, present, and future. Building partnerships between donors and organizational leaders, they increase the number of donors who view organizations not simply as recipients of gifts, but as top philanthropic priorities for themselves and their families.

PREPARING FOR THE ROLE

Nothing better prepares CDOs for the role of culture shaper than extensive experience working with donors. Knowing how donors are likely to react, and then taking the time to factor that knowledge into discussions with CEOs, colleagues, and staff, CDOs strengthen organization-donor partnerships and lead their organizations to substantially greater fundraising results.

Begin with the Language of Partnership

The development profession is replete with words and phrases that distance and even depersonalize the philanthropic partners on whom nonprofit organizations depend, such as "prospect," "target," "moves management," and "low-hanging fruit."

Even the use of first- and second-person language—"*I* would like *you* to give *your* money to the project that *my* colleagues and *I* have designed"—creates an unnecessary and unproductive distance. In shaping the language of gift proposals and in preparing senior leaders for gift discussions, a partnership approach emphasizes

- shared objective as opposed to need;
- mutual respect over ability to impress;
- mutual benefit over donor indebtedness;
- trust over persuasion; and
- results, not just gratitude.

Focus on your language and the attitude with which you interact with donors. In meetings and proposals, use language that respects and incorporates the objectives and interests of donors.

Use Ears and Mouth in the Right Proportion

As in every relationship, listening is critical. A trustee listened to a friend, someone who had no degree from the trustee's institution, talk about how he and his family wanted to give back to the neighborhood where he grew up, the same neighborhood of the trustee's university. The friend also said he wanted especially to focus on fundamental needs of the neighborhood, such as children's health. That led to a great philanthropic partnership; the donor and the university came together to build a children's hospital, and eventually the donor added a pediatric emergency room and then a center for children and specialty care.

"Most presidents and CDOs just don't stop talking," says Reynold Levy. "Approach donors knowing at least as much about them as you do about your institution, then listen, rather than talk. And definitely don't lecture!" Remember the words of Epictetus: "We have two ears and one mouth so that we can listen twice as much as we speak."

Be Honest

Treating donors as potential philanthropic partners always means being completely honest with them, and sometimes this means losing a gift. Institutions sometimes twist themselves into something they are not in order to "get the gift." If an institution is unable to follow through on the objectives of the gift, such a gift will fail, and the donor's belief and confidence in that organization will be damaged if not destroyed.

Sometimes it is best to help donors fulfill particular philanthropic objectives by directing them to other organizations better positioned to partner on those objectives. Donors who trust CDOs and their teams are much more likely to come back, and their next gifts may well fund high-priority objectives for which the CDOs' organizations are the perfect partners.

ADDITIONAL WAYS TO PREPARE

- Build donor relationships that involve multiple representatives of your organization. If your donor knows two people well, introduce a third.
- Start giving and volunteering if you are not already doing so. It is critical to know what it feels like to be "on the other side of the table."
- Get to know your organization's most consistent donors. They will teach you things about the organization that even the CDO and CEO may not know. Learn more about the largest gifts to your organization. Who made them? Who was involved? What led to the gift decisions? What did the donors say about their gifts?
- Get to know other leading philanthropists and understand their motivations for volunteer service and giving.
- When visiting prospective donors, ask them what they hope to accomplish through their philanthropy. You'll have begun by complimenting them, placing them in the category of "philanthropic person," and you will learn a great deal about what matters to them.

NOTES

1. Seymour, *Designs for Fund-Raising*, 6.
2. Alison Sider, "GSB Nets $300 Million Gift from Alumnus David Booth," *Chicago Maroon*, November 7, 2008, http://chicagoma-

roon.com/2008/11/07/gsb-nets-300-million-gift-from-alumnus-david-booth.

3. "A Kid from Peabody High School," *Tepper Magazine*, Fall 2004, 14.
4. "Aspen Music Festival and School Announces $25 Million Gift, Largest in Aspen History," Aspen Music Festival and School press release, December 3, 2007.
5. "Aspen Music Festival and School Announces $25 Million Gift."
6. Jerold Panas, *Mega Gifts* (Emerson & Church, 2008), 117.
7. Joan O'C. Hamilton, "New Institute to Tackle Extreme Poverty," Stanford Business Magazine Online, www.gsb.stanford.edu/news/bmag/sbsm1201/seed.html.
8. Stephanie Strom, "Couple Donate $150 Million to Fight Poverty in Developing Nations," *New York Times*, November 4, 2011.
9. Panas, *Mega Gifts*, 53–54.
10. Levy, *Yours for the Asking*, 36.
11. John W. Boyer, *The "Persistence to Keep Everlastingly at It": Fund-Raising and Philanthropy at Chicago in the Twentieth Century*, Occasional Papers on Higher Education XIII, the College of the University of Chicago, 13.

Chapter Three

Strategist and Planner

Effective annual and long-term planning allows nonprofit organizations to fulfill their missions while maintaining excellent short- and long-term fiscal health. Today's boards expect—and increased external scrutiny requires—CEOs, chief financial officers, and other senior administrative leaders, including CDOs, to employ sophisticated and responsible financial and business planning practices.

Successful CDOs maintain close connections with internal financial leaders and planners, recognizing that these relationships are a key component of their role of strategist and planner. "Since the development office is a major revenue center for the institution, the financial operations teams will have significant interest in the effectiveness of and output from the fundraising office," says Martin Shell, vice president for development at Stanford University. "Additionally, the institution's executive leadership and trustees rely heavily on the chief financial officer and other financial officers for accurate and consistent revenue projections. CDOs always work to ensure there is a close alignment between what development offices report as gift revenue and what financial offices and auditors recognize. This is essential to the credibility of the CDO and the fundraising enterprise."

CDOs also serve as bridges between financial officers and external constituents with an interest in the financial health of their organizations. "Today's CDOs must be financially literate, able to serve as interpreters between chief financial officers, chief investment officers, and external audiences," says Susan Washburn. "Successful CDOs are knowledgeable and conversant on the subject of nonprofit business planning and financing, not simply fundraising goals and progress." Weakness in any area of financial management damages an organization's ability to raise money; CDOs capable of understanding and explaining their organizations' overall financial positions can help prevent or minimize adverse impact on fundraising when financial challenges and setbacks occur.

Successful CDOs understand the business models of the individual sectors in which they work, whether education, health care, arts, or social services. "I am expected to understand the financial drivers of my institution and of peer institutions, as well as the factors that affect the business model of higher education in my state and nationally," says Kassandra Jolley, vice president for institutional advancement at Spelman College. "Shifts in business models have a tremendous impact on development programs."

CDOs who have great facility with numbers instill confidence in board members and senior colleagues. By contrast, those who are unsure of or unable to articulate goals, progress, and how fundraising goals affect larger organizational goals lose the confidence of those around them. Knowing how to read and interpret numbers also allows CDOs to manage their staff and programs much more effectively, and to change course appropriately and without delay. "I pay very close attention to development reports, organization-wide financial reports, and benchmarking statistics. Numbers tell me what I'm doing right; they also tell me what I'm doing wrong," says Deborah Breen.

Facility with numbers and context is also critical when interacting with donors. "The thing that has changed the most in my 35 years in fundraising is the way that donors look at their gifts," says Mark Kostegan. "Today's donors see their gifts as investments, and they want quantifiable impact. They also expect me to be able to compare Mount Sinai to other institutions, placing our overall performance and planning, not simply our fundraising, in a competitive context."

CDOs ensure that development planning integrates fully into organization-wide planning. "When an organization is discussing a significant potential programmatic initiative, fundraising is likely to be important," says Robert J. Zimmer, president of the University of Chicago. "The chief development officer's input cannot be limited to projections on what can or cannot be raised. Fundraising potential and strategy are part of a constellation and fabric of considerations, and the CDO must be able to understand the interplay of considerations and participate in the larger strategic decision-making process." Jared L. Cohon, president of Carnegie Mellon University, agrees, adding, "Effective CDOs appreciate and develop an understanding of institutional interests that are greater than any particular office's interest."

CDOs and CEOs find appropriate ways to engage donors in planning as well. "Especially in recent years, I've found that my role in fundraising is as much talking about strategy and direction—bringing potential funders in to seek their advice and get their input, as well as to educate them, during the planning process," says Laura Walker, president and CEO of New York Public Radio.

Organizational planning falls into two categories: annual planning and long-term planning. Annual planning responsibilities include

- participating in organizational annual business planning and budgeting;
- leading corresponding development annual business planning and budgeting; and
- assisting with audit.

Long-term, multiyear planning responsibilities include

- participating in organizational long-term planning;
- facilitating inclusion of ideas from leaders across the organization and communication with those leaders;
- leading corresponding development long-term planning; and
- contributing to investment planning.

ANNUAL BUSINESS PLANNING AND BUDGETING

Until assuming the role of CDO and senior officer, development professionals' experience with annual business planning and budgeting is limited and focused on building personnel and program budgets designed to reach as much fundraising potential as possible with a reasonable return on investment. CDOs play a significantly larger organizational role, looking at the overall business plan and budget and ensuring that annual development plans support the specific annual needs of the organization. They participate in making difficult decisions about allocation of resources, balancing investment in development with investment in other areas including those directly related to delivery of service, such as teaching, patient care, or arts programming.

Securing Resources for the Development Program

Chief financial officers and other budgeting and planning leaders want and need CDOs to succeed; CDOs are responsible for one of their organizations' largest revenue streams. Chief financial officers and CEOs are predisposed to allocate resources to efforts that lead to increased resources and financial flexibility. Wouldn't it, then, always make sense to invest a dollar wherever more than a dollar can be returned? Why, therefore, do so many CDOs run into difficulty when asking for increased resources for the development program?

CDOs cannot request investments in development programs in the hope that "someday" the investment will pay off. Organizations cannot afford to invest in development based solely upon an assessment of potential. Whether the projected return is short term, long term, or both, and whether it is unrestricted, restricted, or both, investments in development should be based upon solid plans integrated with overall organizational plans.

"CDOs who are thriving are the ones who can make a strong business case for investment in fundraising," says Beth Herman, principal, EBH Consulting LLC. Jim Thompson agrees: "CDOs should seek out board leaders, administrative leaders, programmatic leaders, and anyone else who brings planning expertise, and work with them to build a strong business plan for the advancement enterprise itself. That plan, aligned with overall organizational planning, should guide all the CDO's budgeting, programming, and hiring. If done right, everyone owns a piece of the business plan and feels responsible for its success." Nonprofit organizations deserve nothing less, and board members and other donors will increasingly demand nothing less.

Standoffs regrettably but regularly arise between chief financial officers and CDOs—a request from the latter for additional resources met by skepticism or outright refusal from the former. Most often, the standoff is a result of one or more of the following:

- a weak relationship between the CDO and chief financial officer;
- an unhealthy competition rather than partnership between the CDO and others seeking resources, with the chief financial officer caught in the middle;
- a request for investment of unrestricted resources in the development program to produce an unplanned and/or undesired restricted return, with a corresponding net drain on annual operating funds.

Other senior officers make requests of a chief financial officer aimed at advancing fulfillment of the organization's mission. If they are competing with the CDO for limited resources, the chief financial officer is torn between investments with direct impact on mission fulfillment and investments that might lead to increased resources and thus to increased future impact. This is a lose-lose position that only adds to the stress of the chief financial officer's already challenging job.

A much happier outcome is achieved when other senior officers support and even advocate for increased resources for development. The CDO is no longer shouting in one ear of the chief financial officer while "competitors" for resources shout in the other; rather, the CDO partners with other officers in developing a plan that balances current and potential needs, and presents this *alongside* those partners to the chief financial officer. This kind of partnership is possible, because every other officer is also counting on the CDO to increase fundraising revenue. Moreover, it requires that the CDO and chief financial officer have shared goals with respect to the balance of unrestricted and restricted fundraising revenue.

The key to successful partnership is to spend less time and energy competing for present resources and more energy developing increased understanding of and commitment to shared potential. This involves partnership not only with the chief financial officer, but also with all senior officers. Successful CDOs understand and are committed to the current objectives of colleagues and take the time to develop broad understanding of their organizations' collective potential to provide for future objectives.

They are also excellent stewards of resources that are allocated to development. They acknowledge that every dollar invested in development could otherwise have gone to direct funding of students, or patients, or artists, and they accept responsibility for ensuring a return on investment that justifies this apportionment of resources. In this way, they build trust among colleagues, increasing the likelihood of support for future funding requests, and giving chief financial officers a much better night's sleep.

Hitting the Goal but Missing the Mark

Restricted and unrestricted gifts have very different impacts on the organization's operating budget. Without careful attention to this distinction, the organization might surpass overall fundraising goals and at the same time experience a problematic or even catastrophic budget deficit.

Unrestricted gifts are budget-relieving: They provide dollars that can offset any expense. Organizations place a high value on unrestricted gifts; donors, on the other hand, often want some control over the use of a gift, particularly a large gift. Restricted gifts, unless they are in support of already budgeted items, add expenses as well as revenue; if the expense is greater than the revenue, the restricted gift might actually require the organization to divert other revenue to cover the overall "cost" of the gift.

Gifts restricted to facilities are usually budget-neutral, in that facility renovation and construction is often financed outside of the annual operating budget. Gifts restricted to endowment don't immediately affect the annual operating budget at all; while long-term assets are improved, only the income from the endowment affects the operating budget, and only in future years. Endowment fundraising is a critical part of long-term planning in most organizations, but its limited present impact on annual planning and budgeting must be recognized.

Some organizational leaders will advocate more strongly for endowment, based on their area of responsibility. Others will advocate for funds to support new strategic initiatives for which they have accepted responsibility. Still others will push for unrestricted and other budget-relieving funds. Spending $10 million this year to secure $100 million in new pledges to endowment might sound like a great return on investment, but the effect on the operating budget is a net expense of $10 million with little or no corresponding operating revenue.

CDOs, in partnership with chief budgeting officers, chief investment officers, CEOs, and many other organizational leaders, lead community-wide, ongoing, and ever-evolving conversations about the appropriate balance between unrestricted and restricted giving, short-term and long-term fundraising revenue, and the timing factors, expense, and return associated with each. They assist in creating and communicating goals not only for overall giving but also for each type of giving.

Once senior administrative and board leaders have a shared understanding of the organization's need and priority for each type of gift, CDOs translate these needs and priorities into concrete fundraising goals and explain them to development staff members, volunteers, and potential donors, leading the organization to meet goals in each gift category.

Be Accurate—A Lot Is at Stake

Scott Showalter, vice president of development at the Los Angeles Philharmonic Association, identifies a key difference in the financial responsibilities of a senior fundraising manager below the level of CDO and those of the CDO. "In my fundraising management roles at Stanford University and at the University of Chicago, I participated in setting goals, and then I was held accountable for meeting those goals. Now, as vice president, I participate in organization-wide decisions that rely on accurate financial forecasting.

"If I forecast after the first quarter that we will exceed fundraising goals, the organization will make additional commitments important to our overall strategic objectives. If I forecast after the second quarter that we will raise yet more, we will make yet further commitments. If I need to reduce the forecast after three quarters, I will not be congratulated on having exceeded the original goal; I will have failed my colleagues across the organization who have made organizational decisions based on the higher forecasts."

Before becoming a CDO, Scott didn't worry so much about overprojecting or even underprojecting. He set ambitious goals for his team and did his best to meet them. Most of the time, he exceeded them by a significant margin. Now as CDO, he appreciates more acutely how the overall goals and projections of development have implications in every part of the organization. "Underpromise overdeliver" doesn't work as well anymore—now it means that a critical hire in another part of the organization that could have been made was postponed, and progress in that area was delayed.

Another CDO puts it this way: "If we receive an unexpected $500,000 gift, the organization will likely increase our goal. If we lose three expected gifts totaling $500,000, the organization will count on us to replace them! If we miss our goal, it's my fault. If we exceed our goal, it's not necessarily to my credit—especially if we had a 'windfall' gift. I need to encourage optimistic, sight-raising thinking among staff and donors, but when I get together with my chief financial officer, CEO, and other senior colleagues, I need to be accurate. I'm accountable—the buck stops with me."

One of my earliest and most formative experiences in CDO accountability came in an advisory council meeting, when I was making the case for a substantial increase in investment in the development program. I concluded my presentation with a request for $200,000 in additional funding for the development department and a promise of at least $2 million in additional gifts and pledges *before the end of the same fiscal year.*

Organizations must be able to count on development business plans, and CDOs must have sufficient information to support full confidence in their plans. I had done my homework and knew where we could invest to produce the largest, earliest returns, building the advisory council's and administration's confidence in me and in the development program so that we could begin investing in programs with longer-term yield.

To my complete surprise as well as that of everyone in the room, including the CEO and chief financial officer, an advisory council member got out his checkbook, wrote a check for $200,000, held it in the air next to the CEO, and said, "Since Schiller is so sure of himself, I'll invest in this plan myself, on the condition that he resigns if he doesn't hit or exceed the return on investment he just promised." He looked directly at me, I accepted his condition, and the astonished CEO accepted the check! We increased fundraising results by well more than the amount required, and I learned an incredibly important lesson—*be accurate: a lot is at stake.*

Audit

CDOs can be a tremendous asset to chief financial officers in the audit process, particularly if they are able to communicate with auditors persuasively and have great facility with numbers. Auditors pay close attention to fundraising history, potential, and projections. Organizations and those who audit them benefit from CDOs who are capable of answering questions clearly, confidently, and with a history of accurate goal setting.

LONG-TERM, MULTIYEAR PLANNING

CDOs play an extremely important role in organizational long-term planning. Virtually every plan for growth and improvement will involve additional fundraising revenue. They provide perspective throughout the planning process, allowing organizations to shape plans informed by fundraising potential and challenges. Since CDOs interact with nearly every constituency of the organization, they are in a position to assist in bringing many and diverse voices into the long-range planning process.

"CEOs and chief financial officers rely on their CDO partners to put discipline and process around new projects so they can be packaged and sold," says Laura Walker. That discipline and process includes providing invaluable counsel on the potential for fundraising revenue; the investments in time, education, and other resources that will be required to secure that revenue; and the associated risks. Their plans have clear and quantifiable measurements attached. "Sometimes the enthusiasm of people on the program side needs to be challenged by the CDO," adds Cecile Richards. "The CDO asks the hard questions that donors will ask, and the resulting discussion improves not only the plan, but also the likelihood of success."

Sometimes, CDOs need to initiate long-range planning. Without clear plans, fundraising efforts languish. CDOs who inherit ambitious fundraising goals without compelling strategic plans to support effective fundraising need to ask their organizations to pause and to create those plans. Jon Gossett, as CDO at Houston Grand Opera, inherited a campaign without a strategic plan, and donors, without understanding the intended outcomes of the campaign, expressed concern that the campaign was principally about raising money. Not surprisingly, the campaign stalled. Once a strategic plan was created, and the campaign was tied to that plan, the campaign was successful.

Long-range planning does not necessarily mean endowment planning. Some board members and even administrative leaders jump too early to the conclusion that endowment is the best kind of fundraising revenue, particularly in connection with long-term, strategic program development. CDOs keep the focus on mission fulfillment and help colleagues recognize that sometimes the best long-range strategy is to increase annual, expendable support. Endowments are helpful for long-term financial stability, but a program with insufficient current-use funds may not be worth endowing at all.

Create Long-Term Plans for Development That Integrate with Overall Organizational Plans

"Today's board members expect integrated financial planning in strategy and execution," says Nim Chinniah, executive vice president for administration and chief financial officer at the University of Chicago. "This allows management and board to have a clear understanding of the key drivers that support trajectory. CDOs have to work side by side with chief financial officers and finance committees and be able to hold their own in discussions related to financial modeling."

Successful CDOs possess a detailed and accurate understanding of their organizations' multi-year fundraising potential and multiyear development plans designed to reach that potential. These plans are integrated with overall organization business plans and describe fundraising potential and projections, unrestricted and restricted fundraising potential and projections, budget-relieving and non-budget-relieving fundraising potential and projections, and required investment in fundraising together with projected return on that investment.

Multiyear development plans begin with an assessment of

- the giving capacity of the existing and prospective donor base;
- program maturity: historical performance and performance relative to peers;
- the number and quality of staff and volunteers; and
- resources available for communications, travel, events, and other programmatic needs.

To integrate development plans into overall organizational plans, CDOs lead organizations through an examination of additional questions. These include financial planning questions:

- What is our organizational need for fundraising revenue?
- What do we need in cash each year: immediately available funds?
- What do we need in pledges: funds available over several years?
- What do we need in planned gifts: irrevocable or revocable gifts that may not be convertible to cash for years or even decades?
- What is our need for unrestricted revenue and how much flexibility do we have to raise restricted gifts?
- To what degree should we focus donors and ourselves on immediate needs versus long-term financial strength such as endowment?
- To what degree can we afford to accept gifts for objectives that are important to our mission but not current priorities?
- What additional resources do we need to cultivate and solicit the base properly? What level of return on investment—short term and long term—is acceptable?

Additional questions relate to donor inclination and excitement:

- Have we built internal and external understanding of and consensus around our vision and priorities?
- What is the giving inclination of our donor and prospective donor base—in general toward our organization, and specifically toward our priorities?
- Do we have a clear and compelling case for support? If not, how and when will we develop one?

- Are our plans big enough and exciting enough to inspire the largest gifts we will need? What must we do to raise sights of donors and prospective donors?
- What is the level of belief and confidence among our institutional leaders in our capacity to raise money, and how prepared are they to demonstrate their belief and confidence through giving and asking for leadership gifts? Phrased another way, what do our leaders think a "large" gift is for our organization, are those with capacity to make such gifts inclined to do so, and what must we do to increase this inclination?

With answers to these questions, CDOs lead their development staff members, with guidance from development committees, through additional questions, including:

- How should we prioritize deployment of existing and new resources?
- Understanding that 95 percent of our fundraising revenue will come from 5 percent of our donors, do we know who those donors are likely to be, and do we have sufficient resources focused on them?
- Given that donor decision timelines are not always guided by organizational timelines such as fiscal years, are we providing adequately for unsuccessful and delayed solicitations?

Solid long-term plans give CDOs confidence to make bold requests and bold promises. During my tenure at the University of Chicago, the university more than doubled its investment in development and alumni relations, and we more than doubled fundraising results. Each annual request for additional resources was presented in the context of a regularly updated long-term plan and accompanied by a specific plan for return on investment *within each fiscal year*, and with an explicit promise that future requests would be adjusted based on meeting or exceeding goals for new revenue. Each year, fundraising results exceeded projections, giving the chief financial officer, CEO, and others confidence that precious resources diverted from other potential uses would produce returns that more than justified those investments.

Gifts That Increase Long-Term Assets Yet Reduce Annual Revenue

Planning for steady, long-term growth in fundraising, including campaigns, requires careful and strategic financial thinking across the organization. A CDO at an organization with a budget of $100 million shared the following story: His organization was consistently raising $25 million annually. They were planning to launch a new campaign, with projected fundraising totals in the first year of $30 million—a 20 percent increase over their usual $25 million—and increasing totals in future years. First-year projections included

$20 million in annual fund (cash) plus $10 million in five-year campaign pledges, with $2 million paid on those pledges. This meant $22 million in cash receipts, $3 million LESS than their normal $25 million, on a cash basis.

Some of that organization's largest annual donors were expected to continue annual gifts and add campaign gifts, and others were expected to continue annual giving at a lower level but increase overall giving by making a stretch endowment gift—a priority of the campaign. The plan was a solid one both financially and in terms of stewardship of long-term donor relationships, and total giving over the period of the campaign was expected to increase significantly. However, the plan required the CDO to build understanding and buy-in across the organization, given the temporary reduction in cash flow from gifts that represented a substantial portion of the organization's annual budget.

Gifts That Cost

Lack of proper planning can inadvertently lead to a gift that adds cost, creating a drain on other resources. A CDO shared the story of a board member who was so inspired by the dean's and president's preliminary plans for a new facility presented early in the campaign process that he pledged a large lead gift, and the dean and president accepted.

The feasibility for supporting the new facility had not yet been studied, however, nor were plans for the new facility well formed. In the end, the facility turned out not to be a high priority for the organization, and now, many years later, with limited interest among other potential donors, the organization is struggling to raise the remaining funds needed to proceed with the project.

Incentivize Staff to Do the Right Thing

Without clarity around annual and long-term goals, or without shared understanding regarding the value of cash versus pledges, CDOs risk creating disincentives for development staff. For example: An annual giving staff member's goal is based on unrestricted giving, and a regular $100,000 unrestricted annual fund donor expresses interest in stretching to $200,000 per year for five years to create a $1 million endowment. The annual giving staff member faces unrestricted totals going down by $100,000, even though the organization would be receiving twice as much money. Successful CDOs create incentives that encourage annual giving officers in such a situation to bring their major gift colleagues into the conversation, or to work directly with the donor on the larger gift, even though the gift doesn't help meet annual unrestricted giving goals.

A colleague once played the lead staff role with a donor who made a very large gift to name a performing arts center. The problem was that my colleague was a principal gifts officer in the medical center! Thankfully, one of the first notes of congratulations he received was from the dean of the medical center. The dean recognized that the gift, several times larger than had been anticipated for the medical center, was a great outcome for the university as a whole *and* for the donor.

Investment Planning

CDOs collaborate with chief investment officers and board investment committees with at least two goals in mind:

- to understand and be able to explain to development staff, volunteers, and donors the investment strategies and performance of the organization; and
- to contribute to discussions regarding targets for endowment growth.

Investment planning is a critical part of long-term planning. With carefully established goals for long-term asset growth, CDOs are better able to set annual and long-term fundraising goals that appropriately balance receipt of expendable funds versus receipt of funds restricted to endowment. Growth in endowment also increases the portion of annual revenue that is predictable, adding financial stability. This in turn allows more confident long-term organizational planning.

SUMMARY

Fundraising managers contribute to their organizations primarily by developing departmental plans that *support* overall organizational planning. **CDOs inform** organizational planning. They are indispensable partners to CEOs, CFOs, other senior colleagues, and board members in charting their organizations' futures.

PREPARING FOR THE ROLE

Fluency in business language and best practice helps CDOs more readily relate to board members, major donors, and others who lead their own businesses. Board members serving their first term on a nonprofit board often express their bewilderment at the language and operations of nonprofits. CDOs with excellent business training and experience help board members acclimate more quickly and have a more fulfilling experience.

Even more importantly, familiarity with the principles and practices of successful business administration equips CDOs to create and lead high-functioning and sustainable development programs. "Aspiring CDOs should seriously consider pursuing an MBA. I use what I learned about operations, marketing, and strategy every single day," says Susan Paresky.

ADDITIONAL WAYS TO PREPARE

- Ask to listen in on meetings of your organization's finance committee, investment committee, or long-range planning committee.
- Assist your CDO in annual budgeting. Ask how development's budget fits into the larger organizational budget.
- Assist your CDO in long-term planning for development and, if possible, for the organization as a whole.
- Serve on the board of another nonprofit. Study its budget, profit and loss, and other financial information carefully, and ask its chief financial officer or CEO to explain aspects you don't understand.
- Serve on the board's finance committee or long-range planning committee of another nonprofit.
- Read the *Economist*, the *Wall Street Journal*, and other publications that will help you become more conversant in the language of business and finance.
- Become an expert in the recording and use of data. Accurate and thorough information supports decision making in managing development staff. As a CDO, you will use data in making the case for investment in development, and in supporting strategic positions.

Chapter Four

Trusted Advisor on Board Matters

"When I took my first CDO role, I knew I'd be working much more closely with the board. I had no idea that work related to the board would become one of the largest parts, and a daily part, of my job," says Patricia "Trish" Jackson, former vice president for development at Smith College. Jerry May adds, "Advising on board-related issues has become one of the most interesting parts of my job. Drawing on my graduate work in higher education administration and on many years of experience as a CDO, I contribute thoughts, opinions, and judgments on a wide variety of issues, many of which have little to do with fundraising. It's deeply satisfying to me that my colleagues, especially my CEO, find value in the perspective I bring to these conversations."

CDOs facilitate communication among senior administrative and board leaders. "Effective CDOs bring information and solutions to CEOs about the board, and they provide an alternate way for board members to talk through issues," says Laura Walker. "It is not good if board members see the CDO as someone who just asks for money."

CDOs focus considerable time and attention on the governing board and on many other types of volunteer boards and committees. Their role as trusted advisor on board matters includes

- partnering with CEOs and other senior administrative colleagues in support of board members and activity;
- direct work with governing board and other volunteer group leaders and members; and
- communication related to governance and activity of boards.

PARTNERING WITH CEOs AND
ADMINISTRATIVE COLLEAGUES

CDOs work closely with CEOs, board secretaries, and other senior officers who support the activity of governing and other boards. They

- provide information required for board reports;
- assist in the preparation of budgets and other financial information requiring board review or approval;
- gather data from peer organizations;
- assist with questions of governance structure such as size of board and term limits;
- assist with identification and recruitment of board officers and committee leaders; and
- contribute to CEOs' and board leaders' remarks.

Board Reports

CDOs are responsible for preparation of accurate and up-to-date reports on

- overall fundraising goals and progress—donors and dollars;
- fundraising goals and progress on specific projects of interest to board members, such as campaigns and major strategic initiatives;
- engagement metrics, such as membership or attendance at events; and
- meetings and other activities of development, campaign, and related committees.

They assist with additional reports related to board and board committee activity, including reports on

- identification, recruitment, and retention of board members;
- additions to, and status of, endowment and other long-term assets; and
- long-term planning.

In addition to preparing reports that will be given by CEOs, board chairs, and committee chairs both in committee meetings and in board meetings, they are prepared at all times to give reports if needed, and to answer questions related to the reports. Effective CDOs have an excellent command of the information contained in, and behind, every report, especially information related to numbers. They instill confidence by anticipating and knowing the answers to most questions, or by following up in a timely manner on other questions.

Budgets and Financial Information

Governing boards are responsible for oversight of annual and long-term financial planning and progress. Boards delegate considerable financial management responsibility to CEOs, who in turn depend not only on chief financial officers, but increasingly also on CDOs and other direct reports for responsible and effective annual budgeting and long-term financial planning. CDOs have specific responsibility for fundraising revenue projections and achievement, and they share responsibility for balanced budgets and long-term asset preservation and growth. They do all this in the context of shared responsibility for the mission of the organization: *Financial strength is not an end, but a means to an end.*

Historical Data

Administrative and board leaders appreciate context for the decisions they are called upon to make. Historical data from the organization provide important context, allowing leaders to answer questions such as

- How do this year's goals compare to last year's? To goals of the past five years? Of the past twenty-five years?
- How has our dependence on private support changed over time? Is this rate of change sustainable? Desirable?
- What percentage of our fundraising revenue has gone to current use and what percentage to long-term asset growth, such as gifts to endowment? Are we increasing long-term assets at the rate we require? Desire?

Data from Peer Organizations

Data from peer institutions provide additional context, shedding light on the questions above and also helping administrative and board leaders to answer questions such as

- Will our plans allow us to remain competitive in our peer group?
- Will they allow us to compete at whatever higher level we might desire?
- Do our goals seem achievable, given the experience of peers? Are they more ambitious or less ambitious than those of our peers?
- How might we use the achievements and goals of peers to motivate our constituents?
- Are we setting the right expectations for board members?

A major university asked a potential board member to join the board several years in a row. The potential board member—a man of great wealth—never accepted and never declined. He simply stated that he loved the university and that he would consider the request. At the time, the minimum giving expectation for board members was far below what the donor knew he would be expected to give.

The board, anticipating a new campaign, studied the giving habits of boards of peer universities and, upon learning that peer universities' board members typically carry 20–25 percent of a campaign, came to the conclusion that the average annual expectations of trustees had to be increased dramatically. The nominating committee adopted a goal of increasing the board's collective giving capacity to a level sufficient to cover 20–25 percent of the anticipated campaign. Further, they began talking with prospective trustees openly about this goal.

The previously reluctant prospective trustee joined the board. Increased giving expectations were by no means the only reason, but an understanding that he would not be expected to carry a disproportionate share of giving responsibility made a difference. Board members prefer to be part of a board whose members collectively have the capability to provide leadership in giving. For some organizations, that means 20 percent of total giving, and for others, it might mean as much as 80 percent of total giving. The experience of peers helps boards set the right goals.

In the early 2000s, I worked with an arts organization that was almost 100 years old and was on the verge of bankruptcy. A structural deficit of $30,000 had led to depletion of cash reserves and spending down of most of the endowment. The organization had no minimum giving expectation of board members. Board member giving ranged from $0 to several thousand dollars per member, and totaled only $9,000.

A study of peers revealed board giving expectations of similar organizations ranging from $1,000 to $5,000 per member. The board adopted a minimum expectation of $1,000 for 2003 and a plan to increase that minimum to $2,000 by 2008. Several board members resigned, but most stayed, and clear expectations facilitated recruitment of new board members. A wealthy member of the community, learning of the board's action, pledged $10,000 per year to close the remaining gap, and the organization balanced its budget. By looking at and learning from peer institutions, then increasing the giving expectation of board members, the board led the organization to financial stability.

Governance Structure: Board Size and Term Limits

The availability of board seats for top donors and prospective donors has a major impact on organizational leaders' ability to effect change and drive growth in fundraising. This availability is affected both by size of boards and by the regularity with which seats turn over. For many major donors, board membership is a prerequisite to making an organization one of the top two or three organizations they support financially.

The size of boards varies tremendously from organization to organization, even among very similar organizations. Some nonprofit leaders regard large boards as unwieldy; others see them as exciting and essential to fundraising. My own recommendation is to have a board large enough to accomplish the fundraising required, and small enough to allow the CEO and CDO to maintain personal relationships with all members.

CDOs contribute an essential perspective, assessing and reporting on

- the capacity of the current board relative to the needs of the organization, including the limitations on fundraising, if any, of the current board due to size;
- the importance of board membership to top donors and potential donors not currently on the board, and the potential loss of fundraising, if any, associated with lack of capacity to appoint these donors to the board; and
- the size and composition of boards of peer organizations.

Boards have many responsibilities beyond fundraising, and size cannot be determined by fundraising considerations alone. CEOs and board leaders need information in order to make informed decisions, and CDOs, particularly those desiring change in board size, have a responsibility to gather and provide this information. The most successful CDOs are those who have a full command of the pros and cons associated with board size and can place fundraising considerations in a larger context for their CEOs and board chairs.

Term limits may make it easier for organizations to move unproductive board members off the board and make room for new members. On the other hand, term limits may force an organization to lose highly engaged, generous, and valued members. "But what about the need to get unproductive board members to leave?" asks Michael Kaiser, president of the John F. Kennedy Center for the Performing Arts and advisor to arts boards nationally and internationally. "They should simply be asked to leave. . . . Furthermore," he adds, "it is best to *not* wait even a year or two for a term to end before ridding the board of unhelpful members. Board places are precious; helpful board members are literally worth their weight in gold (or maybe in cash). And unhelpful board members should be removed."[1]

Relationship between Governing and Other Types of Boards

Public organizations, such as public universities, often have institutionally related foundations. Members of these organizations' foundation boards are selected differently from those of their governing boards. The governing

boards are often appointed or elected, and in many instances are more politi-
cally connected than philanthropically capable or inclined.

There can arise a tension between the governing board and the foundation
board because the governing board feels pressure from the foundation board,
whose members are often wealthy business leaders accustomed to making
decisions and donations. One responsibility of the CDO, who may also be the
chief executive officer of the foundation, is to be sure the foundation board
stays focused on its role and does not infringe on the governing board's
responsibility.

The first step is to be sure roles are clearly defined. The nongoverning
foundation board does not "run" the organization and it does not decide
fundraising priorities. Those responsibilities are the domain of the governing
board and the organization's CEO. The foundation board is typically charged
with raising money, investing it to realize maximum gain, and making sure it
is applied exactly as the donor intended.

To ensure no surprises occur for either board, the foundation board should
include a few members of the governing board—not enough to constitute a
voting majority, but enough to be sure the governing board is fully aware of
the foundation's activities, fiscal policies, and procedures. That means the
governing board members of the foundation board should be on the finance,
audit, investment, and development committees as full voting members.

In addition, the CDO is well advised to keep administrative officers of the
organization informed and involved. One way is to make the officers nonvot-
ing "consulting members" of foundation committees that pertain to their
roles with the organization. For example, the treasurer or chief financial
officer might be a member of the investment committee; the vice president
for operations might be a member of the real estate committee and/or finance
committee; the general counsel might be a member of the legal affairs committee. The intent is to keep everyone informed as well as to tap into the
knowledge and strategic wisdom of the staff that serves, primarily, the governing board, but has much to contribute to the foundation board.

Such formal linkages should be augmented by informal interactions between foundation board members, governing board members, and senior
administrative officers, at events, dinners, and receptions. The CDO should
encourage and support an annual joint retreat of both boards, to strengthen
the partnership.

Other boards, such as alumni boards and advisory boards, require careful
attention and coordination with governing boards. Nongoverning board
members want information about governing board activity and appreciate
learning of major decisions in advance of general audiences. Nongoverning
boards greatly extend the reach of the governing board into the larger community. They also provide a pipeline of future governing or foundation board
members and an opportunity for senior administrative officers and board

leaders to learn more about their level of passion for and commitment to the organization.

Recovering from Addiction to Boards

Certain boards are required by an organization's bylaws. Other boards, particularly advisory committees and nongoverning fundraising boards, are often created in order to give top donors and potential donors formal leadership roles. Fundraising-focused boards can be highly effective, particularly when the governing board does not have or accept fundraising as a principal responsibility. But organizations can also become "addicted" to boards, letting the need or perceived need to engage donors serve as the primary motivation for the creation of a new advisory or fundraising committee when other solutions exist.

Creating unnecessary boards or committees leads to heartache on the part of organizations and donors. Staff and volunteer leaders struggle before meetings to create meaningful agendas, and donors resent wasting valuable time and money attending "show-and-tell" gatherings with little substantive discussion.

Experienced CDOs resist creating new boards unless a clear and strong rationale exists for a standing committee. They utilize other, more creative means of gaining donor insight and providing recognition for those who wish engagement beyond giving, including

- informal or formal designation as advisor or councilor, with occasional but substantive discussion between donor and organizational leader, such as CEO or dean, on matters important to the donor, and on matters where the donor's experience or expertise could be especially beneficial; and
- creation of ad hoc task forces with specific charges, and with defined start and end dates.

Board Leadership

The choice and appointment of board leaders is ultimately the responsibility of the boards themselves. Given the frequent interaction of CDOs with board members, however, CDOs are in an excellent position to help CEOs and board chairs identify board members who are most interested in and most suited to leadership roles. Observant, thoughtful, and trusted CDOs make an important contribution to the selection of executive committee members, committee chairs, and chairs of various volunteer groups including the governing board itself. They also assist with smooth transitions in board leadership roles by identifying future leaders early and playing a role in preparing them for their leadership roles.

CEO Remarks to Boards

CDOs sometimes write CEO remarks, sometimes contribute to CEO remarks, and always possess information that could be helpful to CEOs and those drafting their remarks. CDOs, meeting regularly with individual board members and board committees, hear the principal concerns, questions, and ideas of board members. Sharing this information with CEOs enables CEOs to address these issues and helps ensure that board members are getting the information they most need and desire. CDOs also pay careful attention to the communication styles of CEOs so that board remarks, along with all communications, reflect those styles.

DIRECT WORK WITH BOARD MEMBERS

In the words of one university president, "The CDO spends more time with the boss's bosses—the trustees—than any other member of the staff." Peter Meinig, chairman emeritus of Cornell University's Board of Trustees, adds that "CDOs often get to know individual board members even better than CEOs, so their input on issues related to the board is invaluable."

CDOs engage in fundraising discussions with board members and their families, and they support board members in cultivating and soliciting others. CDOs are also responsible for support of development committees, campaign committees, and fundraising event committees. Beyond fundraising-related committees, CDOs work directly with board committees or individual board members to

- identify and recruit new board members;
- engage and retain existing board members;
- steward relationships with past board members, including emeritus and life trustees/directors;
- integrate nongoverning boards and volunteer groups with the governing board;
- facilitate communication between CEO and board members; and
- assist with CEO transitions.

If their responsibilities extend beyond development into areas such as communications, marketing, membership, or alumni relations, CDOs also support the work of committees and individual volunteers focused on those areas. In small organizations without a board secretary, CDOs often play that role as well. In the words of one arts CDO, "When it comes to managing the board, I'm the one, in addition to the CEO. My CEO doesn't have to remember every detail—she counts on me."

"Board members need people they can go to in confidence in addition to the CEO, and in this respect, the CDO plays a critically important role," says Karl Clauss. Effective CDOs are prepared to discuss matters related not only to their responsibilities as chief fundraisers, but also to their broader responsibilities as senior officers and leaders of their organizations.

"Successful CDOs are thought of as much more than 'just' fundraisers," adds Nancy Winship, senior vice president of institutional advancement at Brandeis University. "Their board members view them as key members of CEO cabinets, with shared responsibility for all parts of their organizations. CDOs must be able to converse with trustees and speak their language. They need a firm grasp of challenges facing their organizations and peer organizations, so they can speak with credibility. Possessing a sophisticated understanding of budgeting and finances, they must be able to place their organizations in a realistic but positive light. They cannot speak in clichés and cannot be seen as shallow people who pretend that their organizations are working perfectly." Nancy also notes that effective CDOs are "people that trustees want to speak with on a variety of topics."

Identification and Recruitment of Board Members

One of the most consequential and lasting contributions CDOs make is in the identification and recruitment of governing board members. Board members

- hire CEOs;
- oversee financial planning and asset management; and
- collectively provide a substantial portion—often the majority—of fundraising revenue.

> Many nonprofit boards shy away from being clear about the financial expectations for trustees or keep the price tag low to accommodate incumbent trustees who cannot or will not meet it. This is a terrible mistake. It works an injustice to those served by the nonprofit. When a board sets a higher standard and raises the sights for new trustees even without imposing the same requirements retroactively on others, its giving standards begin to change and the definition of generosity is adjusted upward. And if such a change is combined with significant board expansion, the alteration in the culture of the board and the financial results for the institution improve markedly and very swiftly.[2]

In very close coordination with CEOs, CDOs assist board chairs, nominating chairs, and nominating committee members in setting appropriate expectations for new trustees. Regardless of budget size, organizations depend on their boards for leadership in fundraising. This varies considerably by type of organization: In large universities interviewed, two or three of the top ten gifts each year came from board members, on average, and in small arts organizations interviewed, seven or eight of the top ten gifts each year came from board members. In almost every organization, 100 percent of board members were expected to give annually and make the organizations they served a top priority in their philanthropy. Other potential individual, corporate, and foundation donors pay close attention to board member giving.

When a board adopts clear and specific expectations for leadership in giving, board members more readily assist with recruitment efforts. They are more likely to invite friends and colleagues with significant giving capacity to consider joining the board, knowing their wealthy friends will not be asked to join to make up for the lack of capacity or willingness to give on the part of other board members.

As Si Seymour wrote in 1966, "The philanthropic road sees few travelers who willingly walk alone. Most people, and I would say the rich and relatively rich in particular, usually prefer a parade."[3] This is true of donors at all levels, but it is especially true of board members. Those willing to lead philanthropic efforts have made a serious commitment by joining the board, and they expect others to be with them.

CDOs who are proactive in bringing top donors and prospective donors to the attention of nominating committees are instrumental in elevating the overall giving capacity of their boards. They focus time and attention on this responsibility. They do not wait until the week before a nominating committee meeting to pull together a list of potential candidates. Instead, they build a pipeline of candidates with high net worth and with other characteristics identified by the nominating committee as desirable, and they lead their organizations in systematic cultivation of these individuals.

CDOs do not, however, and cannot bear sole or even primary responsibility for cultivation of potential board members. They are not usually in the same professional and social circles of potential board members. Existing board members are in those circles, and they have the advantage of asking a peer to *join them* in a commitment of time and money that they are making themselves. CDOs have an important role to play, as do CEOs, but CDOs ensure an appropriate balance between their contribution to the process and the essential contribution of existing board members.

Cultivation strategies for board candidates feature

- increased opportunity for informal and formal interaction with the CEO and board members;
- identification of board members in the best position to build relationships—those in the same industry, the same community, or with similar interests;
- establishment of multiple relationships with board members including at least one nominating committee member;

- personal attention, as appropriate, from the CDO; and
- invitations, as appropriate, to exclusive events, as guests of the CEO or board members.

Ideally, by the time candidates are invited to join the board, they will

- be well known to the CEO and to multiple board members, including nominating committee members;
- have a track record of giving to the organization; and
- have demonstrated that the organization is a priority among nonprofits for their time and financial resources—"priority #1 or equal to #2" is a rule used by some organizations.

A systematic approach helps avoid speculative invitations, such as putting someone on the board with the hope that board membership will inspire a substantially higher level of giving. Sometimes such a risk pays off. More often, CDOs and organizations are reminded that hope is not a strategy.

Engaging and Retaining Existing Board Members

"Whatever the motivation, most trustees have certain characteristics in common. They enjoy learning. They treasure meaningful involvement in the vital activities of Lincoln Center. They believe that engagement with it should be fun. Everyone has enough tension and pressure at their own workplaces or in their own families. They do not volunteer to be gluttons for any such punishment in civic life. More than anything else, trustees wish to be respected for who they are and for what they can offer."[4]

Giving of financial resources is very often inversely proportional to giving of advice. Board members giving to full capacity are often annoyed by other board members without giving capacity and those giving beneath their capacity who take an enormous amount of "air time" voicing opinions at board meetings. Asking board members who are not meeting expectations to step down is difficult, but failing to ask them to step down can lead to the loss of highly valued board members.

Board committees allow for meaningful involvement of board members, provided that the members feel ownership of their committee assignments. CDOs and their staff members meet with committee chairs and members between committee meetings, ensuring that each feels needed and supported. In the committee meetings, CDOs do not talk *at* board members. Having prepared the chair prior to meetings, CDOs facilitate discussions in which board members take an active role, and in which the CDO may not participate at all. Committee meetings devoted predominantly to staff presentations are a waste of almost everyone's time and a missed opportunity to build board member engagement.

Stewarding Relationships with Past Board Members

Past board members are usually among an organization's most generous and consistent donors. Given their involvement, they are also among the organization's best prospective donors, especially in life-income gifts, bequests, and other gifts related to the ultimate disposition of wealth. Spouses, partners, and families of past board members are also important prospective donors, too often forgotten as an organization looks relentlessly forward.

In addition, past board members possess a vast amount of organizational knowledge. "There is nothing new under the sun" (Ecclesiastes 1:9). Board members have seen many leaders come and go, many ideas tried and rejected. Wise CDOs seek advice as they consider new approaches and new initiatives. The perspective of past board members should not be considered in isolation—many CDOs have seen good ideas shelved because they've "been tried before and didn't work." Just as often, however, a bad or underdeveloped idea might be greatly improved through the perspective of those who have known the organization intimately and for decades.

Some but not all organizations offer "life member" or "emeritus member" status to past board members. Even when offered, such status rarely goes to everyone, and the status may mean little to nothing in terms of regular and substantive engagement. Current, active board members legitimately receive the most attention from CEOs, board chairs, and board secretaries. Where past board members are engaged, CDOs are usually playing a major role, if not the lead role.

Integrating Multiple and Diverse Volunteer Groups

Organizations feature many types of volunteer committees. Beyond a required governing board, organizations create volunteer groups for

- specific constituencies, such as parent committees, membership steering committees, and African American alumni committees;
- organizational divisions, such as law school advisory groups and cancer department advisory groups;
- functional areas, such as marketing committees and investment committees; and
- special projects, such as gala committees and campaign steering committees.

All of these present opportunities for deepening engagement and commitment on the part of volunteers, and for observing potential for increased volunteer responsibility including service on governing boards. Successful CDOs introduce volunteers to opportunities where they can shine—where they can make an important contribution and enjoy the experience. They also make governing board members, CEOs, and other organizational leaders aware of those volunteers with the greatest potential for governing board membership, so their contributions can be recognized and naturally build toward a more senior volunteer role.

Whether serving on a first-reunion planning committee or on the governing board, volunteers enjoy meeting each other and reinforce each other's commitment. They form lasting bonds with each other, but rooted in the organization, greatly strengthening whatever bonds staff members might create and support. In 2009, the University of Chicago created an annual Volunteer Caucus, to allow volunteers in all parts of the university community across the country to meet each other, share experiences, and support each other's contributions to the university. In its fifth year, attendance exceeded 200.

Facilitating Communication between CEO and Board Members

Board members appreciate and expect open lines of communication with CEOs. Governing boards hire and fire CEOs, so excellent communication between CEOs and governing board members is essential. Alumni board, advisory board, and other board members are also more effective and satisfied when they hear from and feel they are heard by CEOs. CEO-volunteer communication takes many forms, including group presentations, one-on-one meetings, and written communications.

CDOs, generally wearing the hat of "chief volunteer coordinator," ensure regular and effective two-way communication. They keep track of all volunteers and determine, with the CEO, the degree and types of communication required and desired. Most CEOs interviewed, for example, planned at least one face-to-face, one-on-one meeting with each governing board member each year. Given demands on CEO time, it is rarely possible for CEOs to devote this much time to every volunteer beyond the governing board, and CEO communication with these volunteers may more appropriately occur in groups or in written form.

CDOs seen as trusted partners with their CEOs greatly expand the effectiveness of CEOs by serving not merely as facilitators, but also as surrogates for CEOs, facilitating one-on-one communication with a larger number and variety of volunteers. With governing board members, CDOs increase one-on-one contact, and with some individual governing board members, CDOs may have multiple meetings each year.

"The CDO should be able to have comfortable and confidential conversations with everybody on the board, with or without the CEO present," says Adam Weinberg, director of the Whitney Museum. "We are not totally interchangeable, but I want my CDO to be able to represent me, to be my spokesperson, in day-to-day interactions with board members."

Assisting with CEO Transition

CEO transitions, especially smooth and orderly transitions not involving the firing of the outgoing CEO, present special opportunities for fundraising. Effective CDOs capitalize on relationships built by the outgoing CEO, using the deadline of departure to motivate gift decisions. They involve prospective donors with great potential in the selection and recruitment process, if appropriate, and they invite as many top donors and prospective donors as possible to meet the new CEO early, perhaps even before a public announcement is made, building the investment of those donors in the new CEO's success.

CEO transitions also create opportunity for board engagement and recruitment. Potential board members who did not bond with the outgoing CEO may be more inclined to join the board with a new CEO. Existing disengaged board members may become reengaged, especially if they play a role in recruitment or early planning with the new CEO. Outgoing CEOs are also sometimes willing to make some unpopular decisions, helping board leaders transition less productive board members out of active membership.

CDOs assisting with CEO transition do so at a tricky time, understanding that new CEOs may or may not keep an existing CDO in the role, either due to lack of chemistry between the two, a desire to bring a known development colleague into the role, or even simply the desire to choose one's own senior team. CDOs who capitalize on the transition, however, strengthen the likelihood that they will be asked to stay, and win the admiration and appreciation of board members who will assist them should the new CEO-CDO partnership not work.

COMMUNICATION RELATED TO
GOVERNANCE AND ACTIVITY OF BOARDS

Beyond facilitating communication among board members and between board members and other organizational leaders including CEOs, CDOs communicate *about* the decisions and activities of boards with their organizations' wider communities. Decisions and activities of boards affect many people in organizations, and some of those decisions have far-reaching impact. Engaged with every organizational constituency, and aware of their hopes, dreams, fears, and concerns to a degree shared by few others, CDOs facilitate communication about board actions that is as appropriate and helpful to each organizational constituent as possible.

SUMMARY

Fundraisers work with board members as *donors*, and they support them in their capacities as ambassadors and fundraising volunteers. **CDOs** interact weekly, and sometimes daily, with board members, supporting their *overall relationship* with and responsibilities for organizations.

PREPARING FOR THE ROLE

- Serve on the board of another nonprofit. Get as much board experience as possible.
- Study the bylaws and other documents related to the governance of your organization. Compare those to governance documents of other organizations.
- Study the governance structures of nonprofits in your organization's peer group and in your community, particularly those of nonprofits in the sectors of most interest to you (secondary education, higher education, health care, arts, social services, and so on).
- Learn about the expectations of board members in your organization, how these compare to the expectations of board members in peer organizations, how they have changed, and how they are being changed. Ask about what works and doesn't work in initiating, implementing, and supporting increased expectations.
- Get as much time as possible in front of your organization's board and board committees. Get to know individual board members and what matters to them.

NOTES

1. Michael Kaiser, *Leading Roles: 50 Questions Every Arts Board Should Ask* (Brandeis University Press, 2010), 35.
2. Levy, *Yours for the Asking*, 28–29.
3. Seymour, *Designs for Fund-Raising*, 31.
4. Levy, *Yours for the Asking*, 33.

Chapter Five

Thought Partner

Successful CDOs serve as valued and trusted thought partners. Their roles include

- thought partner to the CEO;
- thought partner to colleagues who also report to the CEO;
- thought partner to board members;
- thought partner to donors; and
- thought partner to colleagues across the country (see chapter 8).

Characteristics associated with CDOs considered effective thought partners include intelligence, curiosity, expertise, empathy, giving constructive feedback, and self-confidence.

INTELLIGENCE

"Intelligence" came up as a characteristic of the successful CDO in nearly every interview. Development staff members want their boss to be intelligent in their management and respected as an intellectual peer by other leaders of the organization. Senior officers want a development colleague who will understand the challenges of other units and be able to teach them about development. Board members want someone with whom they can have enjoyable and stimulating conversation and who represents the organization intelligently. CEOs want a thought partner and sounding board. In the words of several development consultants, "Hail fellow well met doesn't cut it anymore."

"CDOs need the intellectual capacity to converse with and relate to their organizations' principals, such as leading faculty members, physicians, artists, researchers, and scholars, and to communicate the essence and importance of their work to people with little basis for understanding that work," says Kassandra Jolley. "The role of CDO has changed significantly in the past 20 years. We can't be just 'the fundraiser' any longer. We must earn the respect of individuals who play leadership roles in a wide variety of disciplines."

CURIOSITY

Another word that came up frequently was "curious." Successful CDOs are, in the words of Susan Feagin, special advisor to the president at Columbia University, "interested in and curious about how their organizations function, who and where the drivers are, where the points of leverage for fundraising can be found." CDOs spend a lot of time with other development professionals, and it's easy for them to lose sight of how they and their programs are viewed. The most successful CDOs meet key influence leaders across their organizations, learning about how the whole enterprise runs while simultaneously learning about and correcting perceptions about how development runs.

They are also curious about the world around them. "Successful CDOs read widely and travel frequently," says Reynold Levy. "They are enormously curious. Presidents and CDOs need to be interesting human beings."

EXPERTISE

In order to serve as effective thought partners to other leaders throughout the organization, in their role as fundraising leader, CDOs must be experts in philanthropy. This entails keeping on top of trends and successful practices, shifts in donor behavior, and the environment for fundraising. "CDOs need to have an ability to analyze changes in the philanthropic landscape and the effect those changes will have on their organizations in the future," says Cecile Richards. CDOs must be perpetual students of philanthropy, the fundraising profession, and the societal context for fundraising, especially as it relates to their own organizations.

CDOs are also expected to have or quickly attain some expertise in the work of the organizations they represent. "Whatever sector I'm in, I need to be knowledgeable about that sector," says Margaret Hunt, vice president of development at New York Public Radio. "I need to know the competitive landscape and how the industry works. When I worked as a CDO in breast cancer research, I needed to talk intelligently about research, researchers, other organizations, and the position of my organization relative to peers. In fundraising, in board recruitment, and in educating my staff, I need to understand how we fit and why we're doing what we're doing. If we're launching a new program at WNYC, I need to understand what others are doing, and why we'll be better."

This does not mean that CDOs develop an expertise on the level of colleagues who have devoted their lives and careers to their work—playing the clarinet, curing disease, or supervising dissertations on the works of Dante. In administrative meetings, in long-range planning, and in preparation for discussions with donors, CDOs who portray themselves as experts beyond fundraising will likely be dismissed as insufferable. Those who instead learn what they need in order to be effective spokespeople, understand the limitations of that knowledge, respect and draw upon the expertise of colleagues, and contribute their own expertise as fundraising professionals will be regarded as important thought partners.

EMPATHY

Successful CDOs are able to empathize. They are curious about the responsibilities, attitudes, and motivations of others. In practicing empathy, they improve their ability to earn the trust and loyalty of staff members and peers, and to understand and shape the motivations of donors. "The most successful CDO I've ever known could sit in any person's seat, figure out what that person wanted and why, and respond appropriately, consistently producing the best outcomes for all concerned," says Carol O'Brien, leading development consultant and president of Carol O'Brien Associates, Inc.

Lack of empathy has led to the downfall of many CDOs. Without empathy, it is very hard to achieve the philanthropic partnership with donors discussed earlier in this book. Beyond examples with a direct and immediate adverse impact on fundraising, CEOs and board members shared dozens of stories of CDOs who failed due to their inability to place themselves in the shoes of internal colleagues. These CDOs, constantly in "command and control mode," tried to force change rather than focus on removing obstacles to change.

A story from a university president helps to illustrate.

> A new professional school dean wanted to achieve greater coordination of development efforts between the professional school staff and the university development staff. With a history of poor relations between the two staffs, and a faculty well aware of this history, the dean needed a solution that would achieve greater coordination and yet be acceptable to the faculty of the school. The dean proposed that the school-based development director have a dotted-line reporting relationship with the university CDO, and a solid-line relationship to the dean. Oblivious to the politics involved and the earnest desire, in this case, for the dean to find a solution that would position everyone involved for the greatest possible success, the CDO insisted on a solid-line relationship

to the university CDO, and a dotted line to the dean. The CDO lost the confidence of all concerned and wound up with no relationship at all.

Within months, the CDO also lost his job.

Above all, successful CDO thought partners know their board members and other donors and what they're thinking, and they bring that information back to their colleagues. "We spend far too much time talking to ourselves," says Curt Simic, president emeritus of the Indiana University Foundation. "We talk *about* what people 'out there' are thinking, but we don't truly know what they're thinking unless we go out and ask them!"

"CDOs must have an ability to understand and predict what board members and other donors will think, how they will respond, what questions they will ask, and what concerns they will have," adds Alan Fletcher. "Middle managers think, 'This is my job, what is the most efficient way to get it done?' Able to empathize, CDOs aim for a result that makes the most sense for both organization *and* donor, choosing the most productive rather than most expedient path."

GIVING CONSTRUCTIVE FEEDBACK

A trusted, empathetic thought partner can share invaluable information that may be difficult to hear. The advancement of nonprofits depends on the successful performance of CEOs and other organizational leaders. "These leaders often step into their jobs with little development experience, but some may not admit that or even realize it about themselves," says Susan Feagin. "Part of the job of the CDO is to give constructive feedback to leaders who are not performing their roles successfully but to whom the CDO may report, because if the CDO doesn't do it, often no one else will. The ability to provide this feedback, that can range from visionary thinking to wardrobe choices, depends upon a high level of mutual trust."

SELF-CONFIDENCE

Newly appointed CDOs must be effective listeners, information gatherers, and relationship builders. They approach new positions and new organizations with humility, eager to learn culture and values. At the same time, CEOs, cabinet members, board leaders, and development staff members want and need new CDOs to put ideas forward, to begin to articulate their own vision with confidence. They were hired, in part, for the experience and thinking they would bring to the organization. "Right from the start, CDOs have to add value, not just be sponges," says Jesse Rosen, president and CEO of the League of American Orchestras. "The best CDOs are able to determine the right quantities of their own ideas to put in front of people, and how and when to do so, at the beginning of, and throughout their tenures."

THOUGHT PARTNER TO THE CEO

Robert J. Zimmer puts it this way: "I expect the CDO to think with me and other senior leaders about the university on multiple levels, integrating development perspective, and then instill that integrated thinking into the development program as a whole. Successful CDOs understand and are able to talk about the larger goals and mission of the organization and lead others to think about and talk about them in a substantive and significant way."

Every new program or initiative has risks, and fundraising is often among the greatest risks. CDO responsibility is not limited to meeting revenue targets; CDOs are sometimes responsible for whether a program succeeds or fails altogether. "We're not usually dealing with questions of life or death," says one CDO, "but the pressure is extreme. I have to be prepared to contribute to the overarching question of whether a new program is the right program at the right time for my organization."

Margaret Hunt says, "Partnership with the CEO is critical to my work. Other successful CDOs I know all have strong partnerships with their CEOs. My CEO and I work closely on donor strategies and relationships, but it's much more than that. We discuss organizational priorities, opportunities, positioning, and branding. Because CDOs are externally focused, we see and hear lots of things that are valuable to our CEOs, including how external audiences perceive our organizations. My CEO and I also discuss how to keep board members engaged and excited, not just as donors, but as contributors in many ways."

"The development leader, an essential partner in raising resources to reach the president's goals, often acts as both 'coach and confidante' in preparing the president for fundraising success. Experts have linked the relationship to a marriage, and personal chemistry counts. However, this union, like any marriage, requires trust, open communication, and work."[1] This partnership must be honest and authentic. "People who pander and say only what they think CEOs want to hear don't make it—CDOs have to be genuine," says Nancy Winship. At the same time, "I want my CDO to be a good advisor and critic of the CEO *to the CEO and not to others*," says James Cuno.

Preparing for effective thought partnership with CEOs requires CDOs to pay close attention to what the board expects of the CEO, to those with the greatest influence on the CEO and on the organization as a whole, and to the CEO's personal style.

Nonprofit CEOs report to governing boards, and governing boards will make the final evaluation of CEO performance and measure of CEO success. Fundraising is in most cases a key component of CEO evaluation, but successful CDOs are aware of all the major expectations coming from the board. The more CDOs can support CEOs in meeting principal expectations, the more CEOs value their CDO partners.

"Several times each year, I reflect on the five influence leaders with the greatest potential to enhance or inhibit the president's success generally and our success in advancement specifically," says Robbee Baker Kosak. Those with the greatest influence change over time and might include board members and other top donors as well as administrative and programmatic leaders, especially those who report directly to CEOs. Government leaders, community leaders, and CEOs of peer organizations can also be among key influencers. CEOs appreciate CDOs who respect the many perspectives and pressures faced by CEOs on a daily basis.

Spouses and partners of CEOs are among the CEOs' most important and influential thought partners. CEOs in some weeks, however, spend more time with their CDOs than they do with their significant others. Beyond time spent directly with CEOs, CDOs also consume significant blocks of CEO time, scheduling donor and volunteer meetings and events that often involve evenings and weekends. Many CEO spouses and partners are also directly involved in relationship building with donors and volunteers. Wise CDOs listen carefully to the perspectives, concerns, and ideas of CEO spouses and partners, if only because they recognize the influence they will have on the thinking and stamina of CEOs.

CEO style is also an essential consideration, and effective CDOs either already possess compatible work styles and communication styles or quickly adapt. "Good chemistry between the president and the vice president of advancement is critical, and the latter's competence and experience won't make up for a personal mismatch," writes Mary Ellen Collins.[2]

Mary Ellen Collins goes on to quote Eric Johnson, vice president for university advancement at Tufts University: "As a member of the president's senior management team, he expects me to be part of thoughtful discussions about everything that's happening at the university, not just fundraising."[3] With this expectation, those involved in the hiring of CDOs, especially CEOs and recruiters, need to pay even closer attention to potential for thought partnership between CEOs and CDOs. This requires looking beyond skills and qualifications, to shared values and approaches to life and work.

In 2012, I worked with Daniel Porterfield, president of Franklin & Marshall College, to recruit a new vice president for advancement. As we began the search, Dan described to me the process he had gone through in recruiting each of his direct reports. With top candidates, he spent as much as ten hours on the phone and in personal meetings before making a final decision. In a search with six top candidates, this could mean as much as sixty hours of Dan's time. Having hired hundreds of people prior to my work in search, I confess I'd never spent anything close to sixty hours of my own time as CDO on a candidate pool for any individual search.

Initially I was concerned that candidates might not be willing to spend so many hours in discussions with Dan, and that this approach might slow down the search. After visiting with Dan's senior team, however, I immediately saw the impact this approach was having on the cohesiveness of his newly forming team. Every vice president who had been through the process noted the powerful and positive effect it had had on his or her decision to come to F&M. Further, during our search, every candidate—the successful candidate as well as those who ultimately did not get the job—expressed great admiration for the amount of time and thought Dan put into these conversations.

His first telephone conversation focused on values, on an exchange of thinking on what the candidate and Dan each felt was most important in their professional and personal lives. The second conversation focused on the college, the senior team, current opportunities, and current challenges, and again Dan was looking for the degree to which candidate and president would share a philosophy on how to approach their work. The third conversation dove deeper into advancement specifically, including how candidate and president thought about communications, about constituent engagement, and about fundraising. In short, Dan spent hours exploring potential for true partnership.

Thought partnership also includes helping leaders anticipate both opportunities and challenges. "The president and board expect me always to be thinking two or three steps ahead about how an audience will interpret and respond to a message," says Robbee Baker Kosak. "My job is to shape messages that are as strategic and yet as sensitive as they can be."

In 2012, I worked with Brent Assink, executive director of the San Francisco Symphony, on a search for a CDO. When I asked Brent about the qualities and characteristics he valued in his direct reports, his first answer was "ability to see around corners." By this he meant the ability to see potential problems early in order to help the organization minimize their negative impact or head them off altogether, combined with the ability to see opportunities early and help the organization capitalize upon them.

THOUGHT PARTNER TO SENIOR COLLEAGUES

Repeatedly, interviewees underscored the importance of healthy and productive relationships between CDOs and other direct reports of the CEO, especially chief financial officers. CDOs and other organizational leaders who enjoy thought partnership with each other take their relationships to a deeper level and have greater impact on their respective programs as well as on their entire organization.

Securing the intelligence, curiosity, empathy, and expertise of colleagues can be of enormous benefit to CDOs. Colleagues bring perspective as fellow senior leaders, direct reports to the same CEO boss, and individuals with acute understanding of the organization's principal opportunities and challenges. They bring fresh eyes and ears to CDOs' opportunities and challenges, while drawing on shared understanding of context and available resources. Ideas on how to remove an obstacle, evaluate a problematic situation, secure additional resources, or reach a particular audience, for example, come from colleagues who may be in a "slightly different boat but rowing in the same current." Particularly when times are challenging, colleagues who not only respect CDOs, but also understand how they think and know that the CDOs reciprocate, are invaluable advisors and allies.

THOUGHT PARTNER TO BOARD MEMBERS

Most board members become involved with a nonprofit organization because they are interested in and inspired by that organization's mission and people. Board members connect with CDOs more often than they connect with most other organizational officials, and board members both want and expect to speak with CDOs about the whole organization, not just fundraising goals and priorities. CDOs need to be knowledgeable and articulate spokespeople on their organizations' work, and on a wide variety of issues that affect their organizations.

Board members, who give a lot of time as well as money to nonprofits, also appreciate CDOs who understand enough about them to help them make their best contribution and have a fulfilling and enjoyable volunteer experience. "Donors respect fundraisers who have done their homework. They enjoy responding to informed questions about themselves and their places of work. They think highly of the intellectually and socially curious, the widely read, the solicitor who has troubled to learn what the prospect is really about."[4]

Board members seek advice from trusted CDOs on matters related to other nonprofits. "Over the years, I have been a sounding board for board members who were on search committees for other nonprofits looking for CDOs, and for board members who were contemplating gifts to other organizations," says Susan Paresky. I have had many similar experiences, including requests for advice from donors with whom I worked many years earlier, in organizations where I no longer have any formal role.

Nancy Winship expands on the importance of reading: "CDOs have to be well read, starting with publications such as the *Economist* and the *Wall*

Street Journal. Magazines like *Trusteeship* are important. Nonfiction books, especially those that trustees might be reading, are important." In addition to helping CDOs support board members in their capacity as volunteers, reading allows CDOs to relate to board members on multiple levels and makes them more interesting conversationalists in a variety of settings, including meals and events.

"The most successful CDO I've ever known stood apart from the rest because she read everything," says Ann Kern, senior client partner at Korn/ Ferry International. "She was highly regarded by all the key players on the board, and they and their spouses loved having her at dinner parties. She knew about history, about business issues, about science, about the arts—she always had something interesting to talk about."

Mary Lou Gorno, University of Chicago trustee and member of the Executive Committee, and Chicago Symphony Orchestra trustee, sums it up: "From a board member's perspective, the role of CDO is one of the most complex and demanding within an organization. It is one of articulating, interpreting, and quantifying institutional vision and priorities to multiple constituencies. CDOs must be insightful, knowledgeable market makers as well as trusted, strategic partners to senior leaders. Board members know that the success of the CEO is highly correlated to the success of the CDO. Board members want engaged, energized relationships with the CDO, as development is one of the few areas where they can become active, high-impact players, expanding upon their policy and oversight roles."

THOUGHT PARTNER TO DONORS

CDOs prepare CEOs and other organizational leaders for thought partnership with donors, and they are well-prepared thought partners themselves. Philanthropic partnership with donors, as discussed earlier in this book, begins with preparation for effective *thought* partnership with donors, and this requires educated, informed listening. The most educated CDO listeners are lifelong students of philanthropic motivation.

Aristotle is often quoted in fundraising conferences: "To give away money is an easy matter and in any man's power. But to decide to whom to give it, and how large and when, and for what purpose and how, is neither in every man's power nor an easy matter." In part, giving decisions are complicated because they are governed by both head and heart. The balance between intellectual and emotional decision making in philanthropy varies widely, from donor to donor, and even from gift to gift. As Blaise Pascal said in the 17th century, "The heart has its reasons which reason knows not."

"When a major donor and a chief development officer sit down to lunch, each is somewhat nervous," says Mercedes T. Bass, philanthropist and leader on many boards. "Development officers shouldn't just start talking about their mission or about a request for financial support. They need to be aware of what is happening in the larger world, know what subjects are of interest to the donor, and be able to open a conversation in a way that puts the donor at ease. The most successful development officers I know go to the theater, read books, and study politics. They ask interesting questions and always have something interesting to say."

The most experienced fundraising professionals assess donor motivation by drawing on their extensive experience in working with hundreds if not thousands of donors. Drawing on this experience, they guide responses to donors, sometimes helping bridge what appear to be impossibly large gaps between donor objectives and organizational objectives.

CDOs also study motivations of the mind and heart that span groups of donors and generations of donors. These include the teachings of organized groups, such as religion, as well as the writings of influential individuals.

Philanthropy has been encouraged and celebrated in religions and other cultural practices throughout the world and throughout history. Studying the wide-ranging contributions of the world's religions, major thinkers and writers, business and civic leaders, and others to this great human tradition gives CDOs a deeper appreciation of the evolution of philosophies and practices of giving and insights into their impact on donor motivation. CDOs study and share with others the richness of thought that has developed over millennia of human experience in this area.

A few examples:

- Hindu Proverb: They who give have all the things. They who withhold have nothing.
- Jewish Proverb: What you give for the cause of charity in health is gold; what you give in sickness is silver; what you give after death is lead.
- Old Testament, Deuteronomy 16:17: Every man shall give as he is able, according to the blessing of the Lord, thy God, which he hath given thee.
- Qur'an 57:18: Indeed, the men who practice charity and the women who practice charity and they who have loaned Allah a goodly loan—it will be multiplied for them, and they will have a noble reward.
- Confucius: A man of humanity is one who, in seeking to establish himself, finds a foothold for others and who, desiring attainment for himself, helps others to attain.
- Thomas Jefferson: I deem it the duty of every man to devote a certain portion of his income for charitable purposes; and that it is his further duty to see it so applied and to do the most good for which it is capable.
- Martin Luther King Jr.: Every man must decide whether he will walk in the creative light of altruism or the darkness of destructive selfishness.

This is the judgment. Life's persistent and most urgent question is "What are you doing for others?"

 The giving philosophies of leading philanthropists have had tremendous impact on the thinking of donors. A recent example is the Giving Pledge, "an effort to invite the wealthiest individuals and families in America to commit to giving the majority of their wealth to philanthropy."[5] Conor O'Clery, in his 2007 book *The Billionaire Who Wasn't*, describes the "profound effect" of Andrew Carnegie's writings on Chuck Feeney, one of the leading philanthropists of our time, especially Carnegie's famous essay "Wealth," first published in the *North American Review* in 1889.[6] "Wealth" is a must-read for CDOs, if only for its influence on the thinking of philanthropists to this day.

SUMMARY

Fundraisers and fundraising managers serve as thought partners to staff colleagues and to some donors and volunteers. Their thought partnership focuses principally on *fundraising and fundraising strategy*. *CDOs* serve as trusted advisors and sounding boards to their CEOs, senior colleagues, and board members on fundraising in the context of *larger organizational strategy and vision*.

PREPARING FOR THE ROLE

- Read! Read what leaders in your organization are reading. Read what nonprofit leaders are reading. Read what donors are reading. Read what nonprofit leaders are writing. Follow authors who are important and influential in the nonprofit sector generally and in fields in which you work and expect to work—such as education, health care, the arts, or international relief.
- Study how your organization and other organizations present themselves in writing. Read mission and vision statements, case statements, and strategic plans. Identify elements and approaches that produce the most clear and compelling presentations.
- Read what donors say about their motivations for giving. See givingpledge.org for letters from many of today's top philanthropists.
- Ask your organization's major donors why they give.
- Give to other organizations, and think about the intellectual and emotional aspects of your decision about where and how much to give.
- Understand your bosses' perspectives and align your work as closely as possible to their approaches and their goals. Evaluate rigorously your

chemistry with your boss and with other senior leaders, in order to be better prepared to evaluate the potential for chemistry with a future CEO boss. Work on putting yourself in the shoes of CDOs and CEOs for whom you work. Learn about the forces that come into play in their decision making.

- Identify the five influence leaders with the greatest potential to enhance or inhibit your boss's success. Identify the five influence leaders with the greatest potential to enhance or inhibit your success. Pay attention to how this group changes over time.
- Anticipate your boss's needs, get out in front of them, and stay in front of them.
- Be an "organizational sociologist." Study the culture of your organization, and get to know how organizational cultures develop and change. Be institutionally fluent, not just knowledgeable.
- Meet CEOs of other organizations and ask them what they most need and want from their CDOs.
- Be intellectually curious. If you don't know, ask; don't fake it.
- Practice empathy. Try to understand others' perspectives and motivations before criticizing. Improve your own openness to constructive criticism from others. Think carefully about the approaches of your critics, the approaches that work better than others, and why.
- Take at least one job working in a development shop considered "world class." Regardless of the level of job you hold, observe what is required for excellence. CEOs and board members seeking transformation of their development programs look for CDO candidates who know from first-hand experience what a leading program entails.
- Make sure that you're an interesting person. If your colleagues don't want to have lunch with you, why would you think a prospective donor would want to have lunch with you? Talking about fundraising is interesting only to a point. Well-developed personal and family interests make you a more compelling lunch or dinner partner.
- When you interview for a CDO role, seek a CEO with a vision you find compelling—a vision you can share and own.

NOTES

1. Mary Ellen Collins, "Bonding Time," a sidebar to "Stick the Landing," *Currents*, Council for Advancement and Support of Education, January 2013, 25.
2. Collins, "Stick the Landing," 23.
3. Collins, "Stick the Landing," 24.
4. Levy, *Yours for the Asking*, 184.

5. See http://givingpledge.org/.
6. Conor O'Clery, *The Billionaire Who Wasn't* (PublicAffairs, Perseus Books Group, 2007), 99.

Chapter Six

Flag Bearer

Successful CDOs are passionate and steadfast flag bearers

- for their organizations;
- for their CEOs;
- for their development programs and staff members; and
- for philanthropy and philanthropists.

They have keen self-awareness, knowing where they are needed and where their particular combinations of skills, talents, experiences, and passions can have the greatest impact. They are purposeful about the organizations they choose to serve, making sure they can fully embrace an organization's mission and leaders before seriously considering a CDO opportunity. Taking these opportunities, they become known as ardent and inspiring proponents of their organizations.

"CDOs are at a high-wire intersection of serving CEOs, board chairs, donors, staff, and volunteers who count on their partnership," says Sandy Sedacca, vice president and chief development officer at Planned Parenthood Federation of America. "On our toughest, loneliest days, our perseverance comes from serving institutions to which we bring deep, personal commitment. And our ultimate privilege and joy come from successes we share, with leaders and teammates, in delivering for the missions we love."

FLAG BEARER FOR THE ORGANIZATION

CDOs must be knowledgeable, articulate, and passionate about the mission, vision, planning, and leadership of the organizations they serve. "The best CDOs I've known have a deep, personal connection with an organization's mission," says Joan Harris, former board chair of the Harris Theater for Music and Dance and the Aspen Music Festival and School. "They understand the way an organization works and the ethos. They relate, intimately, to the passion of board members and top donors, and this allows them to communicate and lead fundraising efforts much more effectively."

Deep commitment to an organization's mission also leads to greater professional and personal satisfaction. "Make sure you are very passionate and can be 1,000 percent dedicated to the essence, history, and mission of the organization you are serving," says Jim Thompson. "You must be its most determined and unflinching champion, regardless of changing circumstances. When you have this passion, you will enjoy your role in the life and future of a great, perpetual organization. It's the greatest job I can imagine!"

Knowledge and Ability to Communicate

"Successful CDOs have a clear understanding of the mission of the enterprise, a clear understanding of the CEO's vision, and a clear understanding of their role in the enterprise, which is to bring their personal and professional abilities to the task of supporting that mission and vision," says James Cuno. "They build excellent relationships with donors firmly rooted in that mission and vision, thereby maintaining the trust and confidence of donors and the CEO."

They also understand the competitive context in which their organizations operate and their organizations' distinctive and important contributions within that context. "It's very important for CDOs to be aware of larger societal forces that shape our organizations today and to be conversant in them," says Daniel Porterfield, president of Franklin & Marshall College. "Ability to situate strategies within larger contexts and trends allows CDOs to articulate the value being added to society."

Equipped with knowledge of the organization and its competitive context, CDOs partner with CEOs and other leaders in shaping and delivering messages that are clear and compelling. "CDOs must communicate with flair and fluency, interpreting a cause or institution in more than pedestrian fashion," says Reynold Levy.

At the same time, their style must be appropriate to the organization. "CDOs need to be culturally and stylistically synchronized with the president, the academic and administrative leadership, the board, and the university community at large," says Andrew Alper, chairman of the University of Chicago Board of Trustees. "Every institution has its own culture, and the CDO must have a deep understanding of that culture and be able to reflect it in appropriate ways to alumni and other donors."

Rather than assuming that their knowledge and experience will be directly applicable to any new setting, effective CDOs meet their organizations where they are. Dozens of CEOs and CDOs shared stories of CDO failure resulting from a "one size fits all" approach. One shared the story of a CDO who referred to how things were done in the CDO's prior institution in nearly every sentence. Besides being irritating, especially to volunteers and donors, the CDO made several missteps applying practices that were completely inappropriate to the organization's culture. Especially as they begin in their roles, CDOs listen and learn, in order to place themselves not merely as development leaders, but as senior leaders within their particular organizations.

They also must set the right tone. "It is important that CDOs understand and appreciate the basic values of the institution, that they know how to sing the institution's song and get it in the right key," says Don Randel. "There must be a certain amount of cheerleading, but that can't get out of hand; it must be appropriate to the institution, its community, and its character."

"It's Not about Me"

"Early in my CDO tenure at one institution, I dined with a charming trustee about my age," says Beth Herman. "He said, 'Your talk was great, and you were right about what we need to build here. But how are you going to do it if you're not one of us?' For a moment, I doubted myself, instantly seeing all the ways in which I was not one of them. I was not an alum, not a lacrosse fan or prep school graduate, not a southerner, not a duck hunter, and not a man in a place where most of the people in power were male. Then, looking at this generous man who loved his school with such passion, I said, 'If this work were about me, I might not succeed. But it's about bringing all of you closer. If you help me learn the culture, I can make an important contribution, because I believe deeply in education and love serving people who support it.' That trustee became my advancement committee chair and best friend on the board."

Passion

Successful CDOs are passionate about fundraising and about the missions of the organizations they serve. The responsibilities of CDOs are complex, challenging, and taxing. Jerold Panas lists several qualities that top givers expect in a fundraiser, summarizing with a characteristic he finds "in all of the great fundraisers: They love their work. . . . It burns like fire in their bones." Without this fire, the work becomes overwhelming and exhausting. Panas continues, "There are the long hours, long days, some of which seem never to end. But still there is joy and exhilaration, fulfillment and an inner glow."[1]

Personal experience with the organization, such as holding a degree from the college or university served, does not necessarily translate into passion and ability to inspire passion for an organization, and lack of personal experience does not prevent a CDO from developing passion. Passion, or ability quickly to develop true passion, is both essential to success and critically important to the resilience required for long-term professional and personal satisfaction in the job.

"I began piano lessons at age 4, and music has been a big part of my life ever since," says Scott Showalter. "Until recently, my career focused primarily on higher education development. Now that I can marry my passion for music with my professional skill set and experience, my daily work is especially meaningful. I spend many evening and weekend hours at the office, and my interest level and staying power are significantly greater because of my fundamental connection with our core business."

A first-generation university student, I matriculated at Cornell University with a generous financial aid package. Without this assistance, made possible by generations of Cornell alumni, it would not have been possible for me to attend Cornell. From my freshman year, I hoped that someday I would have the means to support future students. During four extraordinary years, I had the opportunity to travel throughout the United States meeting Cornell alumni, as a member of the Cornell University Glee Club. We also performed for every alumni homecoming and reunion weekend, and I saw the power of a deeply engaged alumni constituency.

After graduation and a year in Boston, I returned to Ithaca to serve as associate director of choral music and was eventually appointed as an adjunct faculty member in the Department of Music. Another year later, I was invited to join the development staff. For more than five years, I led weekly rehearsals involving hundreds of students, interacted with faculty colleagues in music and other departments, met alumni around the world, and brought all this knowledge and experience, together with my personal gratitude for the financial aid that made it all possible, to my work with donors and prospective donors.

In short, higher education and music opened a world of opportunity for me. My professional life and board service have focused almost entirely on education and music. The story of the impact of scholarship support on my life came up hundreds of times as I worked with donors on literally hundreds of millions of dollars of gifts designated to financial aid. My passion for music has made it rewarding, fun, and easy to talk with hundreds of donors about gifts in support of musicians and musical organizations. Among my favorite fundraising projects were establishing an endowed choral music–commissioning fund in honor of my teacher and mentor Tom Sokol, at Cornell University, and helping to secure a major gift from the Andrew W. Mellon Foundation in support of NPR Music.

There are many important types of nonprofits, and I can appreciate the important roles they play, though I am truly passionate about only some. CDOs sometimes succeed without personal connection to and passion for an organization, by developing an intellectual connection and feeding off the personal passions of others' connections to the organization. For myself, the deep personal connection got me through many challenging and stressful times. In the one instance in my career where I did not have that passion, I found that the reward did not outweigh the stress.

CDOs sometimes experience significant deterioration in health or in quality of family life due to the demands of the job. The job is stressful for everyone, and a great antidote to stress, in addition to a supportive family and a glass of great wine, is a deep, personal connection to the mission—the level of passion that would lead CDOs to give philanthropic resources and volunteer their own time to the organizations they serve or to other organizations with similar missions.

Resilience

"Resilience is critical to success in the CDO role," says Andrew Alper. "Donors say 'no,' volunteers get upset—there are a lot of people who can get mad at the CDO from time to time." Carol O'Brien concurs, adding, "Personal resonance with the mission of the organization goes a long way in giving CDOs the resilience to make it through the challenges of the job."

Cecile Richards strongly agrees. "Because of the adversity she faces, our CDO wouldn't make it without deep commitment to the mission. People have strong feelings about our organization, and most of the time a powerful, personal experience is driving their involvement. The CDO, in order to survive and thrive, must be able to relate to their passion."

Resonance with the Mission Is Much More Important Than Title or Salary

Several CDOs shared stories of chasing a title or salary, only to find that, without deep passion for the mission and leadership, they could not do their best work, they were profoundly unhappy, and they ultimately could not succeed. The most successful CDOs love what they do—not every minute of every day, but enough to sustain them through numerous setbacks and never-ending demands for additional fundraising revenue. Title and salary contribute to self-esteem and quality of life, but their appeal fades quickly if not backed up by pride of association with the organization and its people, grounded in a passion for its core mission.

FLAG BEARER FOR THE CEO

CDOs prepare the way for CEOs, positioning their CEOs for success with a wide variety of constituents. CDOs meet with top donors and prospective board members before their first meetings with CEOs, educating them not only about an organization's mission, but also about the CEO and the CEO's vision and planning. Successful CDOs promote their CEOs at all times with all constituents.

Recognizing the degree to which their CEOs will be evaluated based on success in fundraising, CDOs credit their CEOs' vision, planning, and cultivation and solicitation capabilities whenever and wherever possible. They play to their CEOs' strengths, allowing them to shine, succeed, and enjoy their roles.

FLAG BEARER FOR THE DEVELOPMENT PROGRAM AND STAFF

CDOs hire and support outstanding fundraising professionals. They remove obstacles, allowing their team members to do their very best work. They unfailingly promote and defend their staff members, quietly removing those whose performance does not meet the needs or expectations of the organization. They share news widely of successes large and small, constantly building confidence in the development program and in the organization as a whole. Continually they make the case for uncompromising excellence in development with the CEO, colleagues, board leaders, and other volunteers and donors.

One of the most important ways in which they "carry the flag" for the development program is by securing resources that provide for first-rate work. Nonprofit organizations cannot afford to compromise in the hiring and support of faculty members, physicians, and artists. They deserve similarly accomplished and capable development professionals, and CDOs must create an environment that supports recruiting and retaining an appropriate level of talent. Certain positions require competition in a local or regional market, and other positions require competition in a national market. CDOs are acquainted with that market and partner with human resources officers and talent acquisition managers to stay abreast of the market and maintain their competitive position.

FLAG BEARER FOR PHILANTHROPY AND PHILANTHROPISTS

CDOs educate those within their organizations who view fundraising as a "necessary evil," and they remind everyone in their organizations of the fundamental importance of philanthropy to past, present, and future success.

They position donors as essential partners in creating the futures of their organizations and engage as many people as possible in the joy and satisfaction associated with well-cultivated, solicited, and stewarded gifts. "If nonprofit leaders don't . . . come to embrace fund development as a central and valuable part of their work, rather than an unpleasant distraction, fundraising success will continue to elude too many organizations."[2]

There are many wealthy people; only a fraction of them are philanthropic. Philanthropists are people who have decided that they have enough for themselves and their families and that they want to do something meaningful for their community with what is left over, whether that is $5 or $5 billion. Their community might be geographical, people with shared experiences such as cancer survivors, or interest-based, such as a group of opera enthusiasts or nature lovers. CDOs know, seek out, and build relationships with philanthropists. They are philanthropic themselves. They introduce colleagues to philanthropists, and philanthropists to other philanthropists. They love philanthropy and philanthropists, and it shows.

SUMMARY

Fundraisers derive personal as well as professional satisfaction from *raising money* for organizations in which they themselves believe. **CDOs** apply their commitment to mission far beyond their work with donors. They assist in shaping organizational planning and vision that are deeply rooted in mission. CDOs *believe in their organizations and leaders and instill that belief in others.*

PREPARING FOR THE ROLE

- Be philanthropic. Find your passion and support it financially.
- Be a volunteer.
- Engage friends and family in supporting the organization you serve or organizations important to them.
- Read everything published about your organization.
- Reflect on your own level of intellectual and emotional engagement, and potential for that engagement, with your organization and with other nonprofit organizations.
- Eat, sleep, and breathe the mission of your organization. Talk about it!
- Seek positions in organizations with missions and values that resonate deeply with you. Don't chase title and salary in any positions, including those prior to the role of CDO. If you love what you do, those will come. Without that love, the thrill of title and salary fades quickly.

- Know yourself well enough to understand whether your values and an organization's values will be in alignment. If not, you won't fit in, and you won't succeed.
- Build experience in shaping vision, adopting vision, translating vision into words you can own and sell, and promoting vision outside of your own area.
- Practice positioning your supervisor for success. Don't worry if your supervisor, or your supervisor's supervisor, gets credit for something you've done.
- Meet and read about leading, beloved philanthropists. Tell stories to your family and friends about philanthropists and their impact.
- Meet and learn from CDOs known as successful flag bearers.

NOTES

1. Panas, *Mega Gifts*, 114.
2. Bell and Cornelius, *Underdeveloped*, 23.

Chapter Seven

Visionary and Confident Sight Raiser

Frontline fundraisers develop great skill in raising the sights of donors—inspiring them to give larger and larger gifts. Successful CDOs apply this skill more broadly, inspiring great achievement across organizations by raising sights internally as well as externally, including those of staff, administrative leaders, and board leaders:

- They stimulate visionary thinking on the part of those responsible for strategic planning.
- They are highly effective and thoughtful change agents.
- With a thorough understanding of the missions and objectives of their organizations, they help shape creative fundraising objectives that support the mission while energizing top donors and motivating transformational gifts.
- They instill widespread belief and confidence in organizations and in their potential, reinforcing these on a daily basis. They focus on the positive, set and surpass ambitious goals, and rally the troops when confidence or energy wanes.

Sight raising begins with effective communication. "Effective chief development officers communicate clearly, coherently, eloquently, and persuasively—in writing, in one-on-one meetings, and in front of groups," says Jane McAuliffe, president of Bryn Mawr College. "They can walk into any corporate boardroom and be both comfortable and effective. In every setting, they have confidence and poise supported by broad experience and well-developed social skills, allowing them to instill confidence in others."

Sight raising also requires partnership, especially with the organization's most senior leaders. Behind the most successful campaigns, one finds visionary and persuasive leaders in the positions of CEO, board chair, campaign chair, and CDO, without whose shared ambition and courage little can be accomplished. When such a team comes together, organizations make giant leaps in fundraising achievement.

CDOs encourage everyone around them to raise their sights, and they inspire others to join them in the challenging and difficult work of change. CDOs hire individuals who share their aspirations and who are capable of spreading a sense of possibility. They also roll up their sleeves and work hard alongside their colleagues. "The most effective sight raisers are also Sherpas—they know the terrain, guide others, and carry a lot of the weight themselves," says MaryJane Kubler, founding partner at KublerWirka.

STIMULATING VISIONARY THINKING

In his book *Mega Gifts*, describing the motivation behind gifts in excess of $1 million, Jerold Panas writes, "And note this well. Big and bold programs sell. Major donors want to soar to heights others have not reached, or cannot reach. They give to dreams and visions that glow."[1] Later in the book, he adds, "Men and women don't give to needs. They give to dreams and dazzling visions."[2]

CDOs must be ambitious for their organizations. In order to inspire increased giving, they must stimulate visionary thinking among programmatic leaders across the organization that will engage and excite donors. "Successful CDOs raise sights of colleagues by drawing out their hopes, ideas, and aspirations, helping people move organically and together toward concepts that have transformational power," says Daniel Porterfield.

They encourage visionary thinking. "All members of our senior leadership team benefit from a CDO colleague who pushes us to aim higher," says Jesse Rosen. "CDOs should be fearless advocates for their vision and their view, ready to claim their position and engage in competing views. Their approach must be civil and respectful, but they should not allow themselves to be shot down easily by others. Well-prepared arguments sharpen the whole team's thinking."

CDOs keep the focus on vision, not on dollar goals. Donors do not care whether an organization has achieved the right number of gifts at each level of a campaign pyramid: one gift of $10 million, three gifts of $5 million, ten gifts of $1 million, for example. CDOs also make sure the vision has broad buy-in. It cannot be their personal vision; it must be a vision shared by leaders who are in a position to implement the vision. They know that once it is clear and compelling, with broad consensus, it is ready to become a vision shared by the donor.

CDOs also apply their visionary thinking to the development staff and program. Robert Hurst, co-chair of the board of the Whitney Museum, chair of the Board of the Aspen Music Festival and School, and chair of the development committee at the Aspen Institute, values CDOs "who embrace and even drive the creation of new technologies and modern approaches to communications and to the recording and application of data on donors and donor relationships." In other words, they are at the leading edge of innovation in the field of philanthropy.

"Nonprofit organizations need to raise money in new ways," says Scott Showalter. "The economy, philanthropic landscape, and tax laws are all changing, while competition for philanthropic dollars is growing. As before, CDOs need to know how to run a state-of-the-art annual fund, major gift program, and institutional giving program. But today they also need to question, test, and apply new fundraising models, and at times they need to work alongside CFOs to develop alternative and innovative funding solutions. It's not enough to do the old stuff well."

EFFECTING APPROPRIATE CHANGE

"Chief development officers need to be able to lead organizations through change, applying imagination, energy, and inspiration," says Robert J. Zimmer. CEOs and other leaders make their marks on organizations in large measure through change. In some cases these changes are required to respond to changes in the external environment, and in other cases the changes are intended to strengthen the organization's competitive position and strengthen its ability to fulfill its mission. The changes may affect only a small part of the organizational community, or they may have significant impact across the organization.

Organizational changes require changes in fundraising strategy, and CDOs know how to adjust. Successful CDOs are experienced, creative, and thoughtful change agents. They are capable of implementing change where and when required, and they avoid change when they recognize that it would be unproductive.

Connect Change to the Core Mission

Change can be exciting and inspire higher levels of giving, but prospective donors sometimes fear or resent a change, particularly when they perceive it to be inconsistent with aspects of the mission or culture most important to them. In many cases, prospective donors' involvement stems from their experiences with the organization years if not decades earlier. Successful CDOs ensure that communication connects plans for the future to the core mission, values, and history of the organization, bringing along those whose financial support is needed and desired.

Balance Innovation and Tradition

"CDOs need to find the appropriate balance for their organization between innovation and tradition, between relevance and nostalgia," says Trish Jackson. "Several years ago, in an interview for the position of director of annual giving, candidate Karen Boehnke asked me what I thought was the right balance between tradition and innovation in Smith's annual fund. It was one of the smartest questions I'd ever heard, and I hired her! Karen, now the CDO at the Spark Program, understood that much of her job would be managing that balance, in seeking to increase annual giving. Our senior team took this question further, discussing the balance of nostalgia for one's own Smith experience versus the relevance of a Smith education today in connection with all of our marketing efforts, including marketing for the campaign."

Question Established Practices

Visionary leadership includes the courage to question established practices. "When I served in my first CDO role, I constantly heard the words, 'we've always done it that way,' " says Susan Washburn. "As a CDO, and as a consultant, I've always asked, 'Why do we do this?' If the only reason someone can give me is 'we've always done it that way'—I call that a WADITWA—then it's time to reexamine. CDOs—often called chief *advancement* officers for good reason—are charged with effecting change that advances and strengthens their organizations. Successful CDOs sort out what can and cannot be changed, preserving the 'sacred cows' of their organizations and otherwise stamping out WADITWAs."

CDOs also question established myths, the stories that are perpetuated with or without determinable basis in fact, and in many cases have been around for generations. They determine which are true, which are no longer true, and which were never true, validating and celebrating those that advance their organizations, and debunking those that are destructive.

Avoid Unproductive Change

CDOs listen carefully and understand an environment before making changes, never promoting change for change's sake. "We enter into cultures that have developed over decades," says Jon Gossett, vice president and chief development officer at St. Luke's Episcopal Health System. "One really has to pause and reflect, determining what can be changed and what can't, what should be changed and what should not." Numerous CEOs and CDOs shared stories of CDOs who lost credibility early in their tenures by assuming that changes made in past jobs in other organizations would be equally successful in their new environments.

Change cannot be forced or rushed. Attempts to implement change without sufficient understanding and consensus often lead to a backlash that leaves an organization in even worse condition than that which existed prior to the change, along with increased resistance to any proposed future changes.

Applying Imagination, Energy, and Inspiration

When change is understood broadly and embraced as an application of an organization's core mission to an evolving environment, fundraising can flourish. CDOs, along with CEOs, are frequently on the cutting edge of change, and they become expert in leading colleagues and donors through resistance and fear. Applying imagination, energy, and inspiration, they stimulate visionary thinking that provides a strong foundation for fundraising objectives that drive truly magnificent and transformational gifts.

SHAPING FUNDRAISING OBJECTIVES THAT DRIVE TRANSFORMATIONAL GIFTS

When I arrived at the University of Chicago, leaders throughout the organization expressed frustration that the university had never received a nine-figure gift. I asked each leader for ideas that would motivate a donor to make such a gift. With little conviction throughout the organization that such a gift could be secured, very few ideas emerged, and most were simply multiples of a smaller idea: fifty professorships could be endowed for $100 million, for example. Organizations that do not receive gifts on the scale of peer organizations usually do not believe they can or will receive such gifts, and this becomes a self-fulfilling prophecy.

With the leadership of the president, provost, and dean of the college, the university included in its planning the goal of removing the burden of student loans from low- and moderate-income undergraduate students and their families. This goal had substantial financial implications and came with an expectation that the goal would take many years to implement. It was a visionary goal with the potential to motivate a gift that would be transformative for the university.

Not long after a presentation on this subject to the board, a potential donor asked us how much it would cost to accomplish the whole objective—that is, to replace loans with grants for *every* low- and moderate-income undergraduate student, immediately. This gave the development staff and university leaders the opportunity to articulate a nine-figure gift idea. The resulting $100 million gift, at the time the largest in the university's history, launched the Odyssey Scholarship initiative. The $100 million from the donor would replace loans with grants for 15 years, and the anonymous donor and university challenged all alumni and other friends of the university to respond to the donor's gift by building an endowment of at least $150 million by the end of that 15-year period.

The donor wrote, "I give this gift in the hopes that future generations of students will not be prevented from attending the college because of financial incapacity and may graduate without the siren of debt distracting them from taking risks and fulfilling dreams." University of Chicago president Robert J. Zimmer declared that ensuring low- and moderate-income students access to the college "comports with our highest values." The move, he said, is "central to our mission."[3]

Visionary thinking provides a foundation for bold fundraising objectives, and those objectives lead to transformational gifts. Transformational gifts lead to increased belief and confidence and in turn stimulate additional visionary thinking, starting the cycle anew.

BELIEF AND CONFIDENCE

The two principal ingredients in successful fundraising are *belief* and *confidence.* Transformational gifts make a major contribution, but CDOs focus every day on increasing their own and their organization's faith in a bright and strong future. Whether extroverted or introverted, whether realistic optimists or optimistic realists, successful CDOs are confident and they are believers. They are also experts in instilling these qualities in others.

Donors must have belief and confidence in the mission, vision, viability, and leadership of an organization. Such conviction is equally important, and more often missing, among administrators and staff members themselves. These internal leaders must have confidence in the organization's top administrative and board leaders, in its strategy and planning, and in its fundraising capacity. They must believe that it can and will secure the large gifts it needs. They must also trust the donors enough to invite them into partnership in shaping the future of the organization.

"Donors are usually the easiest when it comes to sight raising," says Curt Simic. "Getting an organization's leadership to raise their sights must be accomplished first. Otherwise, donors will sit on the sidelines or gravitate to other organizations with bold vision and leadership."

"Donors who have a history with the organization can be among the most helpful in raising the sights of internal leaders," he adds.

"An organization must be able to describe the impact that philanthropy can have on the organization and the resulting impact the organization can have on the world," says Kelly Kerner, senior vice president for development and alumni relations at Bowdoin College. "Organizations without belief in their potential for impact and without belief that their planning will inspire philanthropy are not positioned for success." In short, without internal conviction, conviction that already exists among potential donors is hard to recognize. It is even harder, if not impossible, to build.

Jerold Panas writes, "Feel and think what it will be like to secure the mega gift. Engage the extraordinary power of the possible. Make a giant leap of faith. If you're fairly certain you won't get a gift, the odds are you won't."[4] Every person involved in the cultivation and solicitation process must approach the process with vigor and hope. CDOs instill a sense of the "extraordinary power of the possible" in leaders, staff, and volunteers.

Success breeds success, and it also builds belief and confidence. One CDO worked for an organization that had never received an eight-figure gift. When such a gift came in, the CEO and board chair told the CDO that the gift could not be counted in the quiet phase of the campaign. Their reasoning was that the gift was an "anomaly." If the gift were counted, the ultimate campaign goal might become too ambitious. Instead of arguing, the CDO and her staff worked on the next eight-figure gift. When that came in, the same CEO and board chair asked, "Who do you think will give the next eight-figure gift?" Their view of the organization's ability to secure eight-figure and larger gifts had changed forever.

Setting Ambitious Goals

Ambitious goals create excitement. The excitement builds on itself, allowing teams of people to accomplish much more than any individual thought possible. In 1987, the director of choral music at Cornell University asked me to lead an effort to take the Cornell University Glee Club to China. I was serving as associate director of choral music at Cornell University and had no formal fundraising training and no idea where to begin. The goal was thrilling, and a graduate student and I rolled up our sleeves and got to work.

We drew up a budget of approximately $80,000, more than double what the Glee Club had ever raised before. The alumni advisory council was nervous, but we persuaded them to let us continue exploring the project, and we never looked back. A year later, we embarked on a life-changing trip for the 54 student and 29 alumni singers, spouses, and friends who took the trip. A media crew traveled with us and produced a one-hour documentary aired on PBS. The trip cost $250,000, and we raised almost $260,000.

Most gifts were $100 or less; hundreds of alumni, parents, and friends of student singers came together to accomplish something few had believed possible. The project introduced me to Cornell's development office and led to my first full-time job in development. Though the dollars seem small now, after participating in multibillion-dollar campaigns, that experience infused my entire fundraising career with a deep appreciation of the power and achievability of ambitious goals embraced by a team with shared resolve and passion.

Another example comes from Deborah Breen. "In my first CDO role, at Northern Dutchess Hospital Foundation, we went to our physicians and other medical staff asking them to support the new campaign at the same level that the medical staff collectively had supported the prior campaign. In the earlier $1 million campaign, the support of medical staff totaled $50,000, or 5 percent. The new campaign was $10 million, so we were asking for a 10-fold increase. This ambitious goal, however, was a shared goal, and 70 percent of the active medical staff collectively gave $2 million—an astounding 20 percent of the campaign."

Set Goals That Allow for Victory

CDOs strive always to set a goal that is sufficiently ambitious to raise sights and fund priority initiatives yet sufficiently conservative to allow for victory. Missed goals dampen excitement and diminish trust in future goals. CDOs walk a fine line in the goal-setting process. Underpromising can lead to inappropriately reduced funding of mission-critical objectives. But over-promising creates revenue shortfalls and reduces faith in CDOs and in development teams.

Leaders must be realistic and not, in the words of one CDO, "fall into the trap of impossible goals." They do not accept ambitious goals without sufficient programmatic aspiration and careful planning behind them. Donors want goals that are ambitious, imaginative, and exciting, but they also need those goals substantiated. Successful CDOs use data to ground all organizational fundraising goals in reality. Wishful thinking does not get the job done.

Restoring Belief and Confidence

"When the child sex abuse scandal hit and became global news in the middle of our $2 billion campaign, people wondered if our fundraising effort should be put on hold," says Rod Kirsch, senior vice president for development and alumni relations at Penn State University. "My campaign chair and I were on the same page, believing that the campaign was more important than ever. Expressions of belief in Penn State through gifts to the campaign have indeed helped restore confidence both internally and externally. We knew we'd have to pause with some donors, but we focused on keeping dialogue open, increasing our number of personal visits, listening carefully, and sticking to our core messages and activities. Penn State is strong—our campaign will finish on time and over goal."

Beware Unsubstantiated Claims of Greatness

Nonprofit leaders frequently fall victim to myopia. They are so passionate about their own organizations that they allow indiscriminate use of words like "best" and "unique" to creep into their vocabulary. Donors want to affiliate with greatness, but they will be amused if not annoyed by unfounded expressions of superiority. Sometimes an organization, or a specific program, has unique qualities, or is indeed the best of its kind in the nation or the world. CDOs test assumptions so that claims of greatness are both bold and substantiated.

As one consultant puts it, "I hear every day from CDOs who are convinced their organization has the world's most important and compelling mission, and that it should be easy to find individual and institutional donors who agree. All I can think to myself is, 'Get in line!' "

Rallying the Troops

Even when all the stars are aligned, when all the right leaders, financial resources, staff, plans, donors, and fundraising goals are in place, energy and confidence can wane. Fundraising is hard work, and it is tiring. Messages that drive record-breaking annual giving one year fall flat the next. The most successful volunteer committee suddenly falls apart due to a change in leadership. A great staff member who loves the CDO and the organization follows a spouse across the country. Sustained fundraising efforts such as five-year campaigns enter the doldrums, as exhaustion from the sprint of a successful launch sets in before the energy created by an impending deadline can be tapped. CDOs renew themselves, whether through exercise, or spending time with family members and friends who lift their spirits, or discovering someone or something in their organizations that injects excitement. Then they rally the troops.

SUMMARY

Fundraisers raise the sights of donors. ***CDOs*** raise the sights of everyone in and associated with their organizations.

PREPARING FOR THE ROLE

• Practice positive thinking. Almost every glass is partly full and partly empty. Don't settle for the empty part, but don't dwell on it either. It is difficult if not impossible to carry negative thoughts about a task and convince others that the task is achievable.

- Set ambitious but achievable goals, and when energy wanes or optimism fades, rally the troops.
- Be proactive in goal setting and in raising your team's sights. At the same time, push back on goals that you do not believe are achievable.
- Bring well-researched alternative solutions to your supervisor when you bring problems or questions.
- Ask why things are done the way they are, and don't settle for WADIT-WAs (we've always done it that way).
- Develop a risk-taking attitude. Informed by the bigger picture, who the competition is, and what the trends are, look for opportunities, and try new things. Study innovation in the field, and bring ideas to your supervisor and your team.
- Study changes that work and changes that don't work. Especially for those that didn't work, find out why.
- Get to know successful change agents, and add at least one to your network of advisors.
- Seek out visionary leaders, and learn what goes into building strong vision. Create a vision that captures the imagination and loyalty of your team.
- If you don't have belief and confidence in your organization or its leadership, you aren't doing yourself or your organization any favor by staying.
- When seeking your next job, make sure you have a high level of belief and confidence in both the organization and its leadership. If your next role is a CDO role, it is essential that you have faith in the CEO and board leadership.

NOTES

1. Panas, *Mega Gifts*, 39–40.
2. Panas, *Mega Gifts*, 129.
3. Lydialyle Gibson, "Epic Quest," *University of Chicago Magazine* 100, no. 1 (September/October 2007), http://magazine.uchicago.edu/07910/features/epic_quest.shtml#homer.
4. Panas, *Mega Gifts*, 139.

Chapter Eight

Talent Magnet

"Chief development officers must be able to attract the right people and give them the motivation required for truly high performance," says Robert J. Zimmer. Successful CDOs surround themselves with talented staff members. They are known for their ability to identify, attract, groom, and retain gifted people. Their staff members are devoted to them, work hard for them, and stay in touch with them for decades.

Recognizing this trait in themselves, and its value to their organizations, these CDOs further strengthen their teams by hiring other talent magnets both as direct reports and into other management positions. They create a culture in which capacity and proficiency is recognized and rewarded. They celebrate mastery wherever they find it, whether inside their organizations, in the larger development profession, or beyond. Far from being threatened by other accomplished individuals, they seek out those with greater talents, and they are not afraid to single out high performers. Moreover, they introduce experts to their colleagues and to their teams. They may only hire some, but they endeavor to learn from all.

It is important to note, however, that while they hire people who share their values, they in fact seek out those who bring different and complementary skills and perspectives. They enjoy a healthy debate, encouraging colleagues who disagree with them to speak up, creating an environment in which the best ideas win. That said, they are also quick to remove any individuals who choose to weaken or destroy the bonds within the group. Their goal is clear—to create a strong and effective team.

Executive search consultants know these CDOs: Recruiting for them is a pleasure, and trying to recruit staff members away from them is nearly impossible. Sadly, they also know CDOs who are the opposite of talent magnets. They describe in vivid detail unsuccessful development programs marked by fear, mediocrity, and micromanagement. Every consultant could name at least one; unfortunately they are not rare, and they repel. Their manner not only encourages current staff to leave; it also discourages talented individuals from accepting positions.

CDO talent magnets succeed by

- creating a culture that celebrates proficiency and supports winning teams;
- recruiting and retaining brilliant direct reports who share their values; and
- building a network of savvy advisors for themselves and for their teams, both inside and especially outside their organizations.

A CULTURE THAT CELEBRATES TALENT AND SUPPORTS WINNING TEAMS

Top CDOs create a culture in which team members consistently deliver excellent performance. Their teams view themselves, and are viewed by others, as winners. "Successful leaders articulate their position as one that is instrumental in creating and sustaining an environment in which the best and brightest people can realize their dreams and do their best work," says Reynold Levy. Jerry May agrees, adding that "excellence in the role of talent magnet accounts for the greatest difference between good fundraising teams and great fundraising teams."

These CDOs consistently

- hire the very best people, and promote top performers by creating flexible career paths that allow for growth and retention;
- approach their roles with humility, empowering team members, welcoming dissenting opinions, giving credit to others, freely admitting personal mistakes, and taking responsibility for the team;
- remain calm and centered, removing negative energy and those who create it;
- celebrate success and make winning fun; and
- stay connected to team members, engendering care and concern among team members for each other's well-being.

Hiring Top Performers

CDOs set parameters and secure resources required to hire the very best people. They build effective relationships with executive search professionals who come to know them and what they most value in team members. They engage human resources officers, educating them about the highly competitive market for development professionals, and gaining their support and partnership in overcoming challenges.

With their direct reports, CDOs set the tone for recruiting and are clear about expectations:

- They make it clear that managers should never settle for a candidate simply to fill a vacancy.
- Recognizing that excellence is hard to find, when a search produces two outstanding candidates, they do their best to hire both, even when only one position is open.
- They balance consensus and trust. They engage a sufficient number of colleagues in recruitment to ensure that the team gains a comprehensive understanding of a candidate and that the candidate gains a comprehensive understanding of both the position and the organization. Yet they limit the number involved to demonstrate to colleagues and to candidates that team members trust each other's decisions.
- They establish qualities of the team that go beyond skills and aptitudes required for each specific position. My team at the University of Chicago looked for candidates we would be willing to invite to barbecues in our backyards. Senior managers regularly told me this simple concept helped them distinguish between their top two candidates, when one might look better "on paper," but their gut told them the other was the right person for the team. As I think back on the best hires I've made in my career, every one of them passed the "backyard barbecue" test with flying colors.

"Successful CDOs take the time to educate human resources partners on the unique demands of staffing a professional development shop," says Eric Loomis, senior assistant vice president and chief human resources officer in the Advancement Division at the University of Rochester. "Accomplished development officers are in high demand, and they will be chased by opportunities almost from the moment they start in a new job. Successful shops plan ahead and build candidate pipelines like they would prospective donor pipelines."

Susan Washburn agrees. "Your organization's human resources leader can be your best friend or your worst enemy." Colleagues in human resources who understand the highly competitive recruitment market for gifted development officers help CDOs create the titles, compensation packages, and professional growth opportunities required to attract and retain the best people. Where appropriate, they help them engage executive search consultants. "A strong, respectful partnership can be highly beneficial. A weak relationship results in recruitment delays, penny-pinching salary negotiations, and unnecessary conflict," she adds.

A highly compensated development officer capable of managing a program that generates millions of dollars in revenue is more valuable than a moderately compensated development officer whose leadership results in

considerably less. CDOs pay careful attention to hiring and do not compromise; their success depends on their team's success, and their team's success
depends on the quality of every team member. They partner with human
resources experts, but they never abdicate ultimate responsibility for hiring
decisions.

Retaining Top Performers

Too many development program leaders make the mistake of paying more
attention to hiring than to retention. Talent magnets, by contrast, pay very
careful attention to retention. Knowing that they have hired excellent people,
they "re-recruit" their top performers daily, year in and year out. In addition,
rather than keeping top performers in jobs they no longer find challenging,
simply to avoid having to refill the positions, successful CDOs discuss
growth paths, adjust responsibilities to create growth within current positions, and create new positions, where appropriate, to continue growth paths.

They encourage their best people to look at other positions and talk openly with supervisors about why another position might appeal. This open
dialogue lets employees know that their career growth is important to their
supervisors, and it gives supervisors a chance to rethink job descriptions and
structures proactively, rather than having to scramble to retain someone who
already has one foot out the door.

Empowering Teams with Humility

"The person that can create an empowered team will have much greater
impact than the lone actor," says Daniel Porterfield. More than saying, "I
believe in you," successful CDOs give their team members tools, guidance,
and support, allowing them to become change makers and impact makers
themselves.

"One of the biggest weaknesses I've witnessed in CDOs is the feeling that
they have to know it all and be able to cover all the bases," says Kelly
Kerner. "As soon as CDOs realize that a feeling of 'knowing it all' is a
weakness, and not a strength, they're better managers. Staff members who
know the right answer as often, or more often, than CDOs are doing what
CDOs pay them to do!"

Achieving and executing the role of CDO requires great self-confidence.
But the best way to lead is to be someone whom others want to follow. That
requires humility. "Setting yourself up as a big shot and acting like you're a
big shot because you have a big title is a recipe for failure," says Curt Simic.
"The more humble someone is as they ascend in leadership, the better
they do."

One way that CDOs demonstrate humility is through freely giving credit to others. In the words of Harry Emerson Fosdick, American pastor (1878–1969), "It is amazing what you can accomplish if you do not care who gets the credit." Successful CDOs focus more on recognizing everyone who played a role in success than on garnering credit. They see themselves as successful through the accomplishment of others.

Martin Shell tries to "give everyone appropriate credit when things turn out well, and take responsibility myself and for my organization when something fails. Some of the best teachable moments occur following a defeat." Taking responsibility for the team, CDOs never throw or allow senior managers to throw staff members under the bus.

Removing Negative Energy

"The leader's energy affects the whole team," says Elizabeth Herman. "Calm, centered leaders, who have identified and addressed their own fears, can lead their teams through extraordinarily challenging situations. Those who run around with their hair on fire fry themselves and everyone around them. Far from attracting talent, fear-driven CDOs repel talent, and they often repel donors as well."

CDOs encourage others, especially senior managers, to remain calm and centered. They quickly remove staff members who inject negative energy. Asking a negative staff member to resign lifts an enormous burden from the team. Sometimes negative individuals have lost optimism, energy, and perspective due to a long tenure. Asking them to leave is especially painful, but removing noncollaborative and nonproductive individuals is critical to the morale of the team. As a wise board chair advises, "I've never regretted asking someone to leave too quickly, but I've often regretted waiting far too long."

Celebrating Success and Making It Fun

"The most successful chief development officer I've ever known and worked for was able to lead large numbers of fundraisers and support staff emotionally and persuasively toward a common goal," says Carmen Creel, director of development at the Philbrook Museum of Art in Tulsa, Oklahoma. "Working hard toward that goal was always fun; people were never trudging. He consistently and publicly celebrated group achievement, recognizing and thanking every member of the team when a goal was achieved or surpassed. He took the time to call out people in all areas, including administrative assistants, gift processors, and data entry folks. He was authentic in his relationships with everyone, so team members always felt heard; we always felt important in his presence. These qualities inspired all of us to work even harder, to feel more invested, and to feel a sense of ownership in final outcomes."

The more a team wins, the more a team wins. Successful CDOs set ambitious but achievable goals, allowing the fundraising team to win. They also set many short-term as well as long-term goals, allowing for daily victories, large and small. They celebrate these victories, praising staff members and other colleagues privately as well as publicly.

One fundraising shop has a bell that is rung every time a gift agreement is signed, and staff members flock to the bell to celebrate with their colleagues. Fundraising is endless work—the new fiscal year starts the day the old one ends, and it is not uncommon for a new campaign to begin the day after the old one ends. The CDO gives everyone a chance to stop for a moment, recognize a job well done, and refuel for the work ahead.

CDOs cannot, however, be aware of each win of individual staff members and departments. Successful CDOs therefore ask managers both to celebrate individual wins and to notify CDOs so they can make others aware. Each week, CDOs find a significant win or two to bring to the attention of the CEO, board leadership, and the entire development team. Regularly sharing good news boosts morale and builds the feeling that development is a winning team.

If the CDO doesn't toot development's horn, no one else will. This doesn't mean that CDOs should become insufferable braggarts. But CDOs can do an enormous amount to raise confidence both in and within the development team, simply by highlighting successes on a regular basis.

One CDO reported on an experience from her time as an aspiring CDO that will forever shape the way she responds to her own staff: "When I landed a very large gift, I called my CDO from the car, on my way back to the office. I was so excited! I asked, 'Who's your favorite development officer?' He replied, 'I don't have one.' I said, 'You do today!' And he said, 'No, actually, I don't have one.' I didn't need him to hug me, but who does that? You never forget when that happens. He regularly took all the fun out of achieving great things."

Maintaining Personal Connection in a Caring Environment

Successful CDOs manage up and across, but not at the expense of managing down. One consultant shared the story of a university where a sitting dean was appointed vice president for advancement. The president had not been able to find a vice president with a professional development background, and he knew and trusted the dean. Several staff members told the consultant, "He's the president's vice president, but he's not our vice president." The consultant's view was that this had less to do with his background than with his lack of attention to the staff. The university hit its campaign goal, but extremely low staff morale led to the resignation of the vice president.

CDOs with great personal charisma who are used to managing through personal interaction sometimes stumble when they move into roles requiring supervision of a large team. CDOs with teams that can fit in one conference room feasibly can interact with each team member every day or week. Team members feel directly connected with CEOs, board members, and other senior leaders, with only one degree of separation in the person of the CDO. Managing a large team, however, requires a structure that supports a strong sense of connection, even without direct, weekly interaction between CDOs and all staff members.

"Leaders who jump from managing a small team to an exponentially larger team regularly fail," says Timothy Higdon. "A leader with experience only with small teams was hired to lead a team of nearly 75. She lacked knowledge of leadership systems and structures, ability to hire strong senior staff and delegate, and capacity to maintain focus on the big picture. She did not have experiences upon which to draw nor was she willing to trust and empower her staff, feeling that she needed a greater level of professional knowledge, skill, and experience than everyone else on her team in order to be their leader. Ultimately, she was terminated."

Personal charisma remains important, but CDOs in large shops need to build structures that allow for effective delegation and excellent two-way communication throughout the development organization's hierarchy. The telephone game, in which a message is passed along a chain of people and usually comes out dramatically different at the end of the chain, illustrates the challenge in communication within large teams, particularly when complex messages are involved. Effective CDOs pay constant and careful attention to the level of engagement throughout the organization. They are often known to "wander the halls," reinforcing the importance of each team member's contribution and testing the degree to which the visions they have set for their development organizations are understood and embraced by all.

Development is a challenging field. No one understands that better than a colleague. As CDO, I ended every staff meeting by thanking my colleagues for their care and support, and by encouraging them to take care of themselves and each other.

TALENTED DIRECT REPORTS

The most important hires CDOs make are their direct reports. CDOs are given a mandate when they are hired, a mandate that may require sustaining, improving, changing, or eliminating various programs and approaches.

Direct reports must be on the same page as their CDOs, or be able quickly to get themselves onto the same page. This does not at all mean that CDOs should not listen to direct reports as they shape their plans, but once plans are made, CDOs need direct reports who are fully on board. Direct reports also must share cultural values with their CDOs and work every day to instill and reinforce those values throughout their development teams. Those who cannot do this must be replaced, and the sooner the better.

Direct reports should be both prepared and trusted to stand in for CDOs in virtually any meeting with any person. Some may love the role of #2 and have little or no desire to assume a future CDO role; others will aspire to the role of CDO. By hiring and grooming direct reports capable of succeeding them, CDOs strengthen the potential for internal succession and stability. This in turn strengthens the development profession as a whole.

Variety among Direct Reports

Successful leaders hire people who complement their skills and talents, who do things well that they do not do well themselves. "When you read Aesop's fable, do you identify more with the tortoise or the hare?" asks Tim Child, vice president of institutional advancement at the J. Paul Getty Trust. "If the hare, make certain you have a tortoise at your senior table. If the tortoise, make sure you hire some hares! Complementarity is an essential ingredient in generating the kind of constructive and creative tension necessary for a leadership team's success."

Extending Personal "Touch"

As CDOs manage larger and larger teams, and as they are pulled into broader institutional leadership roles and responsibilities, they have less time for personal interaction with development staff members. Several consultants shared stories of accomplished talent magnets who attracted staff members only to lose them after a short period, as they came to realize that the talent magnets who recruited them had no time to serve as mentors. CDOs need their direct reports, including executive assistants, to prompt personal "touches" that keep them connected with the highest-performing members of their teams. Moreover, they need direct reports who, through their own management style and communication, further strengthen the sense of personal connection with the CDO among all staff members.

Stability among Direct Reports

Excellent relationships with CEOs, senior officers, and board members are critical to CDO success as measured by CEOs. But they are equally important to CDO success as measured by staff members, especially direct reports to the CDO, who are keenly aware of strengths and weaknesses in CDO relationships with other senior leaders. When those relationships are understood to be strong, staff members have much greater confidence in their CDOs and much greater security in their own jobs. This leads to greater retention, stability, and energy in the senior team and consequently in the whole team.

CDOs who don't trust their direct reports spend too much time managing down, and not enough time managing relationships with colleagues and superiors. This weakens their relationships with senior leaders, leading to diminished confidence among their direct reports and a vicious downward spiral. CDOs who settle for weak direct reports, therefore, find themselves overwhelmed. They are required to micromanage, increasingly isolated from key decision makers, and often out of a job.

CDOs who hire well, and then trust and empower their direct reports, multiply their impact on their organizations. They create upward spirals marked by more and more time to spend with key decision makers and top donors, increased results, and greater retention of direct reports and other staff members.

TALENT NETWORK

Successful CDOs surround themselves with talented people. In addition to direct reports and colleagues within their organizations, these include intelligent, accomplished individuals in the development profession, in executive search, in philanthropic circles, and in their broader professional and personal communities. They invest time, energy, and great care in cultivating and stewarding these relationships as they build a lifelong network of support. They contribute to the success of individuals in their networks even as they seek and benefit from their advice and counsel.

"Throughout history, great leaders have surrounded themselves with advisers, mentors, intellectual sparring partners, and confidants. Working with a circle of the best thinkers—as advisers, experts, and questioners—is essential to successful leadership," says Saj-nicole Joni, Ph.D., in a book filled with excellent advice for today's CDO. "Using outside insight does not imply any weakness in your organization's talent pools. And it's not something that can be bought on a moment's notice. . . . Particularly when you are thinking through tough issues, you can't suddenly hire this kind of loyalty, discretion, and access to expertise. You can only build it, one step, one relationship at a time."[1]

Each organization has its unique combination of mission, vision, values, and people. But many of the challenges faced by CDOs have been faced and are being faced every day by colleagues in other nonprofits. "Remember people who have improved your game, who have given you great advice, and stay in touch," says Sandy Sedacca. "You might not need their advice in every job, but keep them in your life. Offer to help them, and share back what their support has meant to you."

I could tell countless stories of the impact of expert advisors on my career and on my contributions as a CDO. They have contributed to the shaping of strategies that allowed my teams and me to overcome obstacles. They have listened when I needed to vent about a difficult colleague, congratulated me on successes, and picked me up when I fell. I've had no greater example of the "loyalty, discretion, and access to expertise" Saj-nicole describes than when I was the victim of a video sting shortly after I announced my departure from NPR.

During a two-hour lunch with individuals who presented themselves as potential donors, I was secretly videotaped. Afterward, the perpetrators used highly selective editing to produce a misleading eleven-minute video intended as a political attack on NPR. Within hours, I had calls of support from three university presidents, dozens of trustees and major donors with whom I had worked, dozens of nonprofit leaders across the country, and scores of former staff members. A former U.S. cabinet member called with the timely advice: "Your friends won't need an explanation and your enemies will never believe one." A respected attorney among my trustee friends immediately offered to represent me and introduced me to a leading media crisis specialist. By the end of the day, I knew I was going to weather the storm.

I made headlines for a day, but thanks to the breadth and depth of my network and an outpouring of affirmation, I remained confident as the truth slowly emerged, buried as it was in the fine print. Three members of my network—a trustee, a development consultant, and a friend then campaigning for U.S. Senate—sent letters to the editor of the *Chronicle of Philanthropy* in support, and my colleague and friend Lois L. Lindauer, who had helped me with dozens of executive searches during my career as CDO, offered me a senior position in her firm.

Talent magnets are known for staying in touch with their best hires for life, well beyond their professional relationships in any given organization. In doing so, they knit together direct reports, other staff members, and accomplished individuals outside their current organizations into a large and self-perpetuating network—a network that supports them, the staff members they have hired and trained and of whom they are most proud, and the profession more broadly.

SUMMARY

Fundraising managers hire people with the skill and talent required to accomplish the goals of their *departments*. **CDOs** attract and retain talented individuals for their organizations and build talent networks that will enhance their career-long impact and strengthen the *development profession as a whole*.

PREPARING FOR THE ROLE

- Be a problem solver. When you bring a problem to the attention of your supervisor, offer one or two possible solutions.
- Remain optimistic, and be known as an optimist.
- When others become agitated, practice restoring calm rather than feeding anxiety.
- Inject positive energy. Every member of a team either adds to the team's energy or detracts from it, and he or she makes that choice in every conversation, every day.
- Take great care in hiring. In the words of one CDO, "You can't fix dishonest, you can't fix stupid, and it's very hard to fix lazy." People who are hungry and driven work hard and inject important energy.
- Hire people who are so smart that you don't mind being the dumbest person in the room! Never settle for a less-than-excellent hire. Hire people who complement your skills and talents. Be confident enough to surround yourself with talented, intelligent people and be humble enough to listen to them.
- Never act as if you're the smartest person in the room in meetings with colleagues and board members. Part of your success has been demonstrating your intellect, knowledge, and experience. Now you will also be able to demonstrate your humility and willingness to learn. Monitor how much time you spend speaking versus listening in meetings; you will learn a lot more by listening. Consider yourself a perpetual student who can always learn much more. It will result in your becoming and being known as a thoughtful, wise, and strategic leader.
- Build networks of support within your organization, across the development profession, and with other nonprofit leaders. Make investments in the success of others.
- Attend meetings of your peers at peer organizations to make contacts and to learn about other successful approaches to development work.
- Don't confuse leadership with power. "Power is like a Chinese finger puzzle—the more you try to assert it, the more stuck you get," says Tim

Child. Leadership is about providing direction, vision, and inspiration, and then leveraging the strength and power of your whole team.

- Lead by example. Model the behavior you want from your best employees.
- Don't throw anyone on your team under the bus—ever.
- Keep yourself and your team focused on principal objectives; avoid or minimize distraction and confusion.
- Discuss your career aspirations with your supervisor, and engage him or her if possible in helping you reach aspirations in your current position and beyond.
- Discuss the career aspirations of staff members who report to you, letting them know that you are invested in their career growth.
- When you receive a compliment for your work, immediately give credit to anyone and everyone who helped.
- Look out for colleagues who are struggling or discouraged. Offer some words of encouragement, or treat them to lunch.

NOTE

1. Saj-nicole Joni, *The Third Opinion* (Cambridge International Group, Ltd., 2004), xiv–xv.

Chapter Nine

Mentor to Future CDOs

"To have people who want to be with you, who come to you saying they want to learn from you, who teach you even as you teach them, and who stay in touch as they go and grow—the privilege to be a mentor has been the most gratifying part of my career," says Curt Simic.

Serving as an active mentor is not necessarily critical to success in any given CDO role, but it is vital to the health of the profession. "One of the reasons we're in trouble today is that we haven't treated mentoring as a critical responsibility of CDOs," says Jerry May, CDO for more than 20 years.

Regardless of their intent, all CDOs serve as mentors, if only through example, and they are often unaware of their impact on staff members and others. Today's top CDOs do more. Contributing to the development of the next generation of leaders, they make mentoring a priority. Some seek out specific teaching moments, while others take selected individuals under their wings for extended periods of time, even decades.

My principal mentors have all shared the same set of characteristics:

- they share thoughts and ideas openly and generously;
- they admit mistakes as freely as they share success stories;
- they talk about their own mentors often;
- they much more readily give credit to others than accept credit themselves;
- they don't take themselves too seriously; and, as a result,
- people want to hear what they have to say.

Future CDOs need effective mentoring throughout their careers in order to succeed, and today's successful CDOs embrace the role of mentor, experiencing Curt Simic's feeling of great reward.

MENTORSHIP IN NINE ROLES

All aspiring CDOs need the opportunity to gain sufficient training and experience in areas *beyond* fundraising so that they will be prepared for and successful in the position of CDO. As they train for and ultimately step into the position of CDO, their mentors help them to excel in each of the roles described in this book.

- *Relationship Builder in Chief:* Mentors teach relationship building, expand relationships of mentees, and reinforce good stewardship of relationships. They steer mentees away from attitudes and behaviors that might have been important in their career growth but need to be softened as a much larger number and variety of relationships must be maintained.
- *Shaper of Culture That Embraces Philanthropic Partnership:* They introduce mentees to philanthropists, expand mentees' knowledge of the larger world of philanthropy, gently correct language and practice that diminishes philanthropic partnership, and teach mentees how to build and change philanthropic culture with great sensitivity to existing culture.
- *Strategist and Planner:* Mentors guide mentees in assessing their own strategic and financial planning strengths and weaknesses, gaining foundational expertise in these areas, and learning how to supplement their own strengths and weaknesses through hiring and through building effective relationships with colleagues and advisors.
- *Trusted Advisor on Board Matters:* They underscore the importance of working effectively with board members and other volunteers, encouraging mentees to become students of best practices and trends in nonprofit governance and volunteer management; exposing them to the distinction between administrative and board roles and responsibilities and the dangers of misunderstood or blurred lines; and giving them as much exposure to board members, committees, and full board activities as possible.
- *Thought Partner:* Mentors establish and exercise thought partnership with mentees; expose them to important and effective thought partners; and encourage them to practice and build thought partnership with colleagues, volunteers, and donors.
- *Flag Bearer:* They knowledgeably, ceaselessly, and passionately carry the flag and insist that mentees do the same.
- *Visionary and Confident Sight Raiser:* Mentors raise sights of mentees, ask mentees to raise others' sights including the sights of the mentors

themselves, and teach mentees how to blend optimism and realism. Unrealistic optimism gets organizations, CDOs, and development teams in trouble every single day. Realism without a healthy dose of optimism lowers sights and leaves money on the table.

* ***Talent Magnet:*** They never settle for mediocrity in hiring or in selecting advisors, teaching mentees how to identify and recruit talent, including how to create an environment that attracts and perpetuates attraction of talent.
* ***Mentor to Future CDOs:*** Mentors encourage mentees to pass along what they have learned, in service to the profession and its future.

IDENTIFYING MENTEES AND MENTORS

Effective CDOs, especially those in development programs with 10 or more staff members, convene direct reports at least annually to identify "rising stars" among the staff and discuss their professional development. They pay particular attention to those ready to move into their first management roles and those ready to move into more senior management roles. Recognizing that they will not have sufficient time or energy to mentor all of these individuals directly, they ask their direct reports to share mentoring responsibilities, thereby increasing the number of staff who can have mentors and at the same time improving the mentoring skills of their senior managers.

DIFFICULT SITUATIONS PROVIDE OPPORTUNITIES FOR MENTORING

CDOs have to deal with many challenging situations privately. Confidential personnel matters, upset presidents, donors who want one-on-one meetings, and other circumstances require personal attention where the addition of a development colleague would be inappropriate. But many situations present a great opportunity to include a staff member with CDO potential.

Some CDOs feel it is their responsibility to protect staff members, sheltering them from governance problems, financial and planning challenges, idiosyncratic behavior of senior officers, upset donors, and disagreements between organizational leaders including power struggles. Exposure to these and similar situations, however, especially with trusted CDOs to frame challenges and demonstrate appropriate CDO responses, provides invaluable learning opportunities for future CDOs.

In addition, including colleagues in meetings that involve difficult situations offers several potential benefits to CDOs:

- Annoyed volunteers, donors, or colleagues may be less likely to express their frustration through anger or personal attack.
- Development colleagues bring additional perspective.
- Development colleagues share the burden with their CDOs.

At the same time, CDOs recognize the potential peril in difficult situations, so they take responsibility for, defend, and protect their direct reports and all members of their teams. CDOs who are swallowed up by organizational politics and/or fail to respond effectively put staff members—particularly direct reports—at risk. In the worst case, a direct report, with little or no control, winds up taking the fall with and perhaps even for an ineffective CDO. In the best case, the ineffective CDO damages the reputation of the development team as a whole and/or loses the opportunity to help direct reports understand the larger institutional leadership role of CDOs.

REMOVING OBSTACLES

Responsible for the performance of the entire development team, the CDO hires strong contributors and gives them the tools and support they need to do their very best work. The CDO also removes obstacles to effective performance, allowing team members to focus as much time and energy as possible on primary responsibilities.

Mentors teach obstacle removal, leading first by example. Mentees cannot flourish without sufficient resources and a healthy work environment, and CDOs take very seriously their own responsibility for creating a supportive environment. At the same time, they engage aspiring CDOs in the process so that they are prepared to remove obstacles for their future teams.

Insufficient or Inappropriate Resources

One of the greatest obstacles faced by new CDOs is insufficient staffing and budget. CDOs stepping into their second or third leadership role are much more experienced and wiser when it comes to identifying resource deficiencies and correcting them in advance of accepting a role or early in their new tenure. CDO mentors show aspiring CDOs how to determine appropriate resource levels, how to build cases for resources, and how to win support among board leaders and administrative colleagues, giving aspiring CDOs a much better chance of success in their *first* CDO role.

Disruptive or Ineffective Staff

It is not only smart to remove disruptive and ineffective staff members sooner rather than later; it is the *responsibility* of CDOs to do so. CDOs do not allow weak performers to harm productivity of the team or destroy the morale of top performers. A valued colleague, knowing that I am a pilot, advised me in aeronautical terms: "When constructing an airplane, one wants wherever possible to increase lift and decrease drag. There are plenty of factors that contribute to drag—the equivalent of headwind, extra weight, or bad weather. Team members whenever possible need to contribute to lift."

Mentors show aspiring CDOs how to remove drag without creating unnecessary additional drag. Very often, ineffective team members are ineffective largely because they are in the wrong jobs, perhaps in the wrong organizations. On a deep level, they are as unhappy as their managers and team members. Frequently, managers who fire out of frustration or anger inadvertently create resentment or fear that temporarily or permanently reduces the morale of other team members. Managers who, instead, decisively but caringly counsel people out of jobs improve the productivity *and* morale of the team and sometimes win the long-term gratitude of the staff member counseled out, especially if that person lands in a much happier situation and feels that the manager helped him or her get there.

Distractions

Distractions abound. They include but are by no means limited to organizational politics and a seemingly unending supply of meetings. The potential for distraction seems to grow exponentially with a step into the role of CDO.

Mentors give aspiring CDOs a whole set of skills that allow them to avoid distraction. They teach them to

- identify the two or three things that really matter;
- maintain personal focus on these;
- keep the team focused;
- say "no" without destroying relationships;
- teach team members to say "no" without adversely affecting organization-wide confidence in the team; and
- find ways to set aside secondary objectives and other good ideas so that they do not overwhelm, but so they are not lost.

EXPOSING MENTEES TO LEADERS

One of the most important aspects of mentoring aspiring CDOs involves facilitating contact with organizational leaders, leading philanthropists, and leaders in the profession. "We have to do a much better job of giving #2s the opportunity to interact with the president and the board," says Susan Washburn. Effective mentoring in this final stage of preparation includes greatly increased exposure to

- CEOs and other administrative leaders, their principal responsibilities, and challenges they face;
- governing board and other volunteer leaders, the support they require, and major governance issues;
- top philanthropists and the motivations behind their philanthropy; and
- thought leaders and leading practitioners in the field of development.

Exposure to Organizational Leaders

CDOs have daily interaction with CEOs and other leaders throughout their organizations. Their staff members, however, may have little or no opportunity to interact with these leaders beyond an occasional greeting, sitting in on a large meeting where leaders are present, or attending a presentation by a leader. CDOs give mentees opportunities for more substantive exchange in which aspiring CDOs can observe leaders' thought processes, better understand the pressures under which leaders operate, and learn constructive ways to inform and guide decision making.

Susan Paresky shared information on a highly selective management-training program she created for sixteen senior development managers at Dana-Farber Cancer Institute. The program was called "CDO U" and included twelve 150-minute sessions. Each session included both presentation and discussion. The goal was for participants to gain a deeper understanding of the role of CDO in the context of the mission and business model of a nonprofit organization. Invited guests included senior leaders from Dana-Farber including the CEO, chief financial officer, and general counsel; panels of communications experts; and CDOs and CEOs from other nonprofits.

Exposure to Volunteer Leaders

Working with board members is discussed at great length earlier in the book. Most CDOs have daily contact with board members, and this level of engagement is usually significantly higher than that afforded or required by any position below the CDO level. When board members want attention, they generally want it from board leaders, CEOs, or CDOs. Though they may have relationships with other development staff members, they expect to have some relationship and engagement with the CDO.

CDOs, given their relationships with CEOs, carry considerable weight in discussions with board members. In board meetings, board committee meetings, and individual interactions, board members want CDOs involved, and often they do not want other staff members present. Given the importance and expectations surrounding these relationships, CDOs easily fall into the habit of dealing with board members on their own, even when the possibility of including a mentee exists.

After mentors and mentees have worked out a plan for increasing mentee exposure to board members, mentees can help CDO mentors by reminding them from time to time to include them in discussions and meetings where possible. Mentors can supplement these interactions by asking selected board members to meet with mentees one-on-one. CDOs must be careful not to waste the time of very busy board members, but some board members will be more than happy to be asked. This is another in the category of things we can ask board members to do for our organizations beyond asking them for money.

Exposure to Leading Philanthropists

Top philanthropists beyond those involved in volunteer leadership roles play critical roles in shaping the future of nonprofit organizations. Many CDOs interviewed pointed out the importance of excellent judgment developed through experience in negotiating with donors at the highest levels. Very large gifts are sometimes transformational, in that they can alter the strategic direction of an organization. Sometimes such a transformation is directly in line with carefully developed strategic planning; at other times a gift involves some modification of existing plans.

Philanthropy is personal. A person's giving decisions may be influenced by upbringing, personal and family values, personal and family financial circumstances, health issues, estate considerations, and a host of other considerations that make each giving decision unique. Each gift presents an opportunity to learn more about why people give. CDOs with broad experience in donor motivation are much better equipped to advise presidents and other leaders involved in cultivation and solicitation activity, including in negotiations around "transformative" gifts. Exposure to top philanthropists, their values and motivations, and negotiations between organizational leaders and leading philanthropists is essential to the preparation of future CDOs.

CDOs often feel it is their responsibility to manage cultivation and solicitation with all board members and top donors. While it is important that board members and top donors feel they have access to CDOs, cultivation and solicitation activity is too often slowed down by the many and competing demands on CDO time. Inviting other senior development officers into the process allows CDOs to mentor aspiring CDOs on how to work with the organization's top donors while keeping cultivation and solicitation strategies on track.

Exposure to Leaders in the Development Profession

Successful CDOs reach out to CDO colleagues and other accomplished development professionals in other organizations across the country as they travel, building a network of trusted advisors they will have for life. They introduce future CDOs to these advisors and ask their network to welcome and support their mentees, especially as those mentees move into their first CDO roles. They encourage aspiring and new CDOs to develop their own networks that will sustain them throughout their careers.

Development officers depend on these networks more than ever when they step into CDO roles. "It's lonely at the top" is a phrase to which most CDOs easily relate. "When I first became a vice president, all of a sudden everyone on my staff laughed at my jokes," says one CDO. "It was the clearest sign that my greater level of responsibility came along with a greatly reduced likelihood of honest feedback!" Successful CDOs consistently point to the importance of support networks that go beyond the people in their organizations.

For 25 years Dave Dunlop has been one of my principal fundraising mentors, and Si Seymour, quoted often in this book, was one of Dave's principal mentors. One of the most rewarding parts of my career has been co-teaching CASE's *Inspiring the Largest Gifts of a Lifetime* conference with Dave, along with two other "disciples of Dave." Each year, as we teach side by side, we discuss the value of long-term relationship building, and we hope that the joy we derive from our own long-term relationships helps to illustrate that value.

CRITICAL MOMENTS IN MENTORSHIP

Sustained excellence in the development profession depends on the willingness of successful CDOs and other fundraising leaders to serve as mentors, especially at three key moments in the career path to the position of CDO: stepping into a first management role, assuming a senior management role, and accepting the position of CDO.

Stepping into a First Management Role

A career in fundraising usually begins on the "front line": working directly with donors, whether through direct mail fundraising, telemarketing, event fundraising, or face-to-face. Development officers focus on individual donors and families, institutional donors such as corporations and foundations, or both. After several years on the front line, successful development professionals typically face a choice of remaining principally on the front line or beginning to take on management responsibilities.

Those who excel in frontline fundraising, however, make essential contributions to their organizations, and many are neither suited to nor desirous of careers in management. In fact, the most successful organizations now provide career tracks to allow frontline contributors to advance their careers without taking on management. For example, in 38 years of service to Cornell University, David Dunlop remained on the front line, creating Cornell's groundbreaking principal gifts program. Turning down offers to serve several organizations as CDO, Dave instead chose, and was supported in his choice, to work directly with donors and volunteers who, over the course of his career, gave and inspired billions of dollars of giving to Cornell. Though he never served in the position of CDO, it is undeniable that his contribution was at least as important as that of any CDO he served.

At this decision point in the career path, when a choice regarding the possible move into a management role is necessary, wise development officers seek guidance. In the decision process, and as they launch their management career, mentoring is essential to their success. An offer to serve in this capacity, coming from an experienced and effective CDO, can make all the difference.

Stepping into Senior Management Roles

For those who excel in management, career growth typically comes through managing larger teams in support of larger fundraising goals. As managers advance to senior positions reporting directly to the CDO, mentors facilitate the deepening of their management and leadership skills, including seeing the "big picture," resilience, team building, and delegation. Mentors also ensure that any gaps in development experience are filled, exposing those being mentored to every specialty area within the development office.

Stepping into the CDO Role

The next transition—to CDO—requires a leap, rather than a step. Development professionals up to and including the level of senior development managers devote 90 percent or more of their time to fundraising and management of fundraising staff. CDOs typically spend less than 50 percent of their time on the same duties, and the rest of their time on a completely new set of responsibilities. Many mentors play important roles up to this point, including parents, teachers, colleagues, consultants, and friends, in addition to CDOs, but as aspiring CDOs prepare for and make the "leap," CDO mentors play a critically important role in giving these new CDOs a running start.

Tough Love

In each of these critical moments, mentors give honest feedback, referred to by many of those interviewed as "tough love." This includes sharing information that may be difficult to hear, including comments on

• personal style, including how to dress;

- standard English, including proper grammar;
- etiquette, including table manners; and
- other issues colleagues are often reluctant to address.

Eventually, mentees will lose the confidence of a donor, a board member, a boss or a potential boss if they do not correct these deficiencies. One candidate for a senior position recently made it all the way to a final round; upon wiping his finger along his plate to gather the last taste of a particularly delicious sauce, he was out of the running.

SUMMARY

Fundraisers and fundraising managers seek mentors and serve as mentors to staff members, friends, and colleagues, in order to learn about the profession and improve the performance of their *teams*. **CDOs** expand the reach and impact of their mentoring, and they pay particular attention to the mentoring of future CDOs. The strength of nonprofit organizations across the country and around the world depends on the willingness of successful and experienced CDOs to *perpetuate excellence in the profession.*

PREPARING FOR THE ROLE

- Observe CDOs. You can often learn just as much from a bad boss as from a good one, and you will learn from observing ineffective CDOs as well as effective CDOs, inside and outside of your organization.
- Be ready to learn, from everyone and anyone. View every constituent, internal and external, as a potential teacher or mentor.
- Identify people from whom you have a lot to learn, and take the initiative to keep in regular touch with them.
- Pay it forward—honor your mentors by taking the time to mentor others.

Appendix A

Call to Action

CDOs depend on the support of many individuals. CEOs and board members are certainly among the most critical, but all in the field of development play a role. It is my intention that readers will be inspired, and perhaps compelled, to do what they can to contribute to the success of those in, or aspiring to be in, the position of CDO. I encourage all readers, especially current and aspiring CDOs, to join the CDO Career Network (www.cdocareer.net).

CURRENT CHIEF DEVELOPMENT OFFICERS

CDOs are so focused on meeting the needs of their organizations and CEOs that they sometimes forget to evaluate whether they themselves are still the right person in the right job at the right time. What began as a good fit may not remain so, especially when shifts in organizational direction cause a CEO or CDO to lose confidence in either the organization or each other. Whenever a CEO or CDO is forced to work around this sort of "disconnect," both the development program and the organization will likely suffer. Therefore, it is important that CDOs recognize when a situation is no longer the right fit, so that they can make a change before any long-term damage occurs.

Additionally, much more validation can and should be done to determine fit, during the interviewing process, especially between CEO and CDO. The story of Dan Porterfield's approach to interviewing, in chapter 5, illustrates one president's solution. CDOs, assisted by search executives, should take great care in assessing whether their particular skills, talents, experiences, values, and approaches to work will allow them not simply to *do* a particular job, but to *thrive* in that job.

Once in an appropriate position, CDOs can further contribute to their own success by

- clarifying expectations for themselves and their development programs among all the organization's leaders, power brokers, and stakeholders, as early in their tenures as possible;
- ensuring that they will meet those expectations by defining and striking a balance between fundraising roles and responsibilities and other roles and responsibilities related to their service as senior organizational officers and CEO partners; and
- creating a departmental structure that reflects that balance, and hiring direct reports and other senior development professionals who complement their skills and talents, allowing them to focus on where they can make their strongest and most important contributions.

Finally, by exposing aspiring CDOs to the larger organizational issues at play while providing appropriate shelter, CDOs can give these individuals the opportunity to gain valuable experience in the types of situations they will confront as CDOs.

NONPROFIT CEOs

Nonprofit CEOs have greater responsibility for fundraising than ever before; thus, they need CDOs with whom they have excellent chemistry. A thorough and thoughtful evaluation of chemistry should happen early in the CEO-CDO partnership, allowing plenty of time for a CEO to recruit a new CDO when the chemistry with the existing one is lacking.

Chemistry, however, is not always immediately evident, and nothing is as valuable as time together to measure and build it. New CEOs should take time to evaluate current CDOs, carefully weighing the value of existing relationships, historical perspective, and performance while assessing potential to build an excellent working relationship. It is critical that they also clarify expectations with their CDOs as early as possible, giving CDOs an opportunity to adjust and respond to

- the full range of what they need and want their CDOs to do as members of their senior teams;
- their own individual styles and preferences; and
- the aspirations they, as CEOs, have for their organizations.

CEOs and CDOs who work exceptionally well together report daily interaction, not weekly or monthly. They continue to spend time together in many different contexts, knowing that every opportunity to observe a CEO's interactions with board members and top donors adds to a CDO's capacity to speak and act in ways compatible with his or her CEO's messages and styles.

CDOs consistently report, and consultants strongly agree, that "a seat at the table" is more important to CDOs than money or title, when it comes to recruitment and retention. CEOs who invite CDOs into organization-wide planning discussions, and who allow CDOs to earn and hold a position as strategic thought partner and sounding board, greatly increase the likelihood of sustaining a CEO-CDO partnership throughout a CEO tenure, and even across tenures in multiple organizations.

To this end, Harry T. Lester, president of Eastern Virginia Medical School, advises CEOs, "Be open-minded. When I first hired Claudia Keenan as my CDO, I thought I was hiring someone to run communications and development. I knew little about development, and she knew very little about medicine. She came to me with so many ideas, and very quickly she became the dean's and my strategic partner. I talk daily with Claudia—not just about big decisions, but about little stuff as well. There are very few decisions we've made in the past five years without consulting her."

BOARD LEADERS

Board members are, or at least should be, among an organization's most ardent, loyal, and generous advocates and donors. Knowing better than most donors the principal opportunities and challenges facing their organizations, and understanding on a personal level the motivations and concerns of the organization's top donors, they are extremely well positioned both to guide and to encourage CDOs. Furthermore, given the length of time they have typically been involved with the organization, they have a greater historical perspective on the development program and on the organization than most administrators and CDO colleagues. CDOs are blessed and deeply grateful when board members take them under their wings.

Primarily, CDOs need board members to play leadership roles in fundraising. The most important of these is leading by example through personal giving. At the University of Chicago, the board of trustees adopted an expectation that board members make the university their "top fundraising priority or at least equal to #2." Regardless of the exact wording, boards help their organizations and their CDOs by agreeing to give at a level that sets a high bar for fundraising from all other individuals. Board members also support success in fundraising through encouraging others to give, whether participating in donor cultivation activities or assisting with solicitation of gifts.

Board members are invaluable to CDOs when they join with them and their CEOs in taking a long view that encourages bold and inspiring thinking with regard to the organization and its possibilities. By sharing their knowledge of the CEO and the organization, they help CDOs understand how to support CEO success and how to be successful themselves. By offering timely words of encouragement, board members help CDOs to remain positive and focused on their task, through good times and bad.

ORGANIZATIONS

CEOs, together with cabinet members and board leaders, must create and sustain environments conducive to excellence in fundraising; CDOs cannot do this alone. Healthy environments require the deep and visible commitment of senior leaders to personal involvement in fundraising efforts.

Organizations must also provide CDOs with a senior role in shaping board membership and expectations, and in annual and long-range planning, if they are to succeed. There must also be ample investment in the fundraising infrastructure so that fundraising can grow. Finally, the organization and its leaders must embrace a culture that accepts and celebrates donors as essential partners in the creation of the organization's future.

THE DEVELOPMENT PROFESSION

We as a profession need to talk openly and honestly about the changing role of CDO. CDOs interviewed by Mary Ellen Collins for the article "Stick the Landing," for the January 2013 edition of the Council for Advancement and Support of Education's magazine *Currents* (page 22ff.), pointed out that the profession needs to offer more training and support for CDOs, particularly for aspects of the CDO role that extend beyond fundraising. We also need to find ways to improve CEOs' and board members' understanding of the changing role, in order to establish appropriate expectations, which will vary by organization. Ideally, we will equip CDOs and CEOs to have more productive conversations during the interview process and to set clearer expectations among all stakeholders early in each CDO's tenure.

Each of us needs to contribute to the conversation. In the late winter of 2012, I had the opportunity to assist Holly Hall, of the *Chronicle of Philanthropy*, with an article devoted to this subject: "Failure of Chief Fundraisers Puts Charities at Risk" (March 18, 2012). In late 2012, I had the pleasure of being interviewed by Mary Ellen Collins in connection with her article cited above. Then, in February 2013, Curt Simic and I co-chaired CASE's Winter Institute for Chief Development Officers. We included CDOs, CEOs, and board members on the faculty and as special guests, discussing the roles and responsibilities of today's CDO. I highly recommend Jon Derek Croteau and Zachary Smith's book *Making the Case for Leadership* (Rowman & Little-field, 2012), in which 10 highly successful chief advancement officers are profiled.

Not all within the field of development can or should set their sights on the position of CDO. We must help rising stars in the profession determine their suitability to the position of CDO and at the same time provide interesting and challenging options for those who are not well suited to the role.

"Within our institutions, and across the profession, we need to spend more time talking about how to maximize the long-term careers for 'A-team' players," says Robbee Baker Kosak. Elizabeth Boluch Wood adds, "Although many career development officers aspire to the CDO role, the requirements of the position may not be the best fit for every fundraiser with a proven track record and requisite years of experience. It's important for us as a profession to understand and communicate what is expected of a successful CDO and for anyone interested in the job to have a well-developed self-awareness. The field also needs financial reward and career tracks for those not interested in the CDO title or set of responsibilities."

Christine Adams, director of development at Phillips Academy, Andover, agrees. "In the past 30 years, I've had the opportunity to serve both in #2 roles and as a CDO. My skills are best aligned with being #2. While I'm capable of working as a senior officer and working with boards, I love raising money and managing and coaching fundraising staff. It took me a long time to learn that. As we think across the profession about training and mentoring, we need to be more disciplined and strategic about describing the differences between senior fundraiser, senior fundraising manager, and CDO, and helping people assess their strengths, weaknesses, and aspirations relative to each. The roles are very different and becoming even more so."

As the size and complexity of development programs have grown, career paths have become harder to chart. "With the explosive growth in the number of nonprofits, the implied hierarchy and seniority of professional titles have become confused and inconsistent," says Carol O'Brien. "A 'Director of Development' can be managing one person or three hundred people." Positions held on the way to the role of CDO vary from sector to sector, and even from organization to organization, in their impact on the experience and skill set of development professionals.

While it is unlikely that we will achieve consistency in the meaning of titles across such a wide variety of sizes and types of nonprofit development programs, we can be more clear about the competencies required of CDOs generally and specific to sectors and sizes of organizations, and about career paths and training opportunities that allow aspiring CDOs to gain the array of competencies they will need in order to achieve their goals.

The position of CDO requires excellence in fundraising and in management, but, increasingly, it requires much more. Training in innovative and successful approaches to fundraising and management will continue to be important. Expanded opportunities for CDOs and aspiring CDOs to learn about other aspects of the CDO role will also be crucially important. These must be paired with efforts to educate those who hire and support CDOs about how they can create an environment and culture in which CDOs are given the organizational support needed for their development programs to flourish.

Appendix B

Preparing for the Role—Words of Wisdom for the Aspiring CDO

I asked all those interviewed to answer the following question: "What are the most important things aspiring CDOs can do or think about as they prepare for the CDO role?" Their advice, along with my own, appears throughout the book under the heading "Preparing for the Role." Here is a summary of that advice, together with some additional words of wisdom.

CHAPTER 1: RELATIONSHIP BUILDER IN CHIEF

- Expect the best in others. Be quick to celebrate success, and slow to criticize.
- Constantly improve relationship-building skills.
- Handle difficult situations in person. Stop firing off unpleasant e-mails.
- Defuse tension and restore calm.
- Don't shy away from difficult donors, difficult colleagues, or difficult situations. Volunteer to work with them, and learn from them. As CDO, you will personally encounter many difficult individuals and situations and will need to advise the CEO in others. The more practice you have, the more often you will succeed at handling them successfully.
- Get to know your organization's power brokers, the key administrative, programmatic, and volunteer leaders. Be a collaborative team player and demonstrate that you respect their roles and contributions. You will spend as much or more time building relationships with these individuals as with

donors and therefore need to learn early on how to identify and cultivate excellent relationships with them.

- Get to know colleagues in other departments and learn about how a non-profit organization works. Many CDOs interviewed had worked for some period in a nonprofit field other than development, such as marketing, admissions, or finance. They cited an understanding of the roles of other nonprofit divisions as a great benefit.
- Volunteer for special task forces and committees that give you the opportunity to build relationships with colleagues outside of your normal circle.
- Serve on your own alumni association as a volunteer.
- Welcome people who challenge your assumptions, and allow them to correct your mistakes and sharpen your arguments.
- Study and practice the art of negotiation.
- Steward your entire team as carefully as you steward donors. Happy and fulfilled employees do a better job, they build healthier relationships with donors, and they stay. Work hard to keep star employees, yet don't be afraid to cut underperformers. Resolve problems creatively, through continuing education, schedule flexibility, and many other benefits; they are much less expensive than toxic morale and a revolving door. Learn to position yourself and your team in the context of a larger framework.
- Learn to manage up, across, and down at the same time, juggling and prioritizing the needs of different groups.
- Identify CDO role models who manage difficult situations and relationships well. Study them, and emulate styles and methods that feel right to you.
- Speak with other senior officers (chief financial officer, chief marketing and communications officer, etc.); ask about the challenges they face and how they think CDOs can help them.
- Create a group of those individuals within your organization or broader community who have similar aspirations, and meet with them regularly to exchange ideas. Invite more-experienced CDOs or senior officers to attend as guest speakers.
- Become known for excellence in customer service. Return calls within 24 hours, if not sooner. Learn to be a great listener and create customer-oriented teams among staff and colleagues.
- Finally, when you interview for a CDO position, be sure that you are a wonderful fit with the CEO. This partnership is critical to success.

CHAPTER 2: SHAPER OF CULTURE THAT EMBRACES PHILANTHROPIC PARTNERSHIP

- Use the language of partnership. Eliminate language that creates distance between donor and organization.
- Become a better listener.
- Be honest with everyone.
- Build donor relationships that involve multiple representatives of your organization. If your donor knows two people well, introduce a third.
- Start giving and volunteering if you are not already doing so. It is critical to know what it feels like to be "on the other side of the table."
- Get to know your organization's most consistent donors. They will teach you things about the organization that even the CDO and CEO may not know. Learn more about the largest gifts to your organization. Who made them? Who was involved? What led to the gift decisions? What did the donors say about their gifts?
- Get to know other leading philanthropists and understand their motivations for volunteer service and giving.
- When visiting prospective donors, ask them what they hope to accomplish through their philanthropy. You'll have begun by complimenting them, placing them in the category of "philanthropic person," and you will learn a great deal about what matters to them.

CHAPTER 3: STRATEGIST AND PLANNER

- Become fluent in the language and practice of business. Consider pursuing an MBA.
- Ask to listen in on meetings of your organization's finance committee, investment committee, or long-range planning committee.
- Assist your CDO in annual budgeting. Ask how development's budget fits into the larger organizational budget.
- Assist your CDO in long-term planning for development and, if possible, for the organization as a whole.
- Serve on the board of another nonprofit. Study its budget, profit and loss, and other financial information carefully, and ask its chief financial officer or CEO to explain aspects you don't understand.
- Serve on the board's finance committee or long-range planning committee of another nonprofit.
- Read the *Economist*, the *Wall Street Journal*, and other publications that will help you become more conversant in the language of business and finance.

- Become an expert in the recording and use of data. Accurate and thorough information supports decision making in managing development staff. As a CDO, you will use data in making the case for investment in development, and in supporting strategic positions.

CHAPTER 4: TRUSTED ADVISOR ON BOARD MATTERS

- Serve on the board of another nonprofit. Get as much board experience as possible.
- Study the bylaws and other documents related to the governance of your organization. Compare those to governance documents of other organizations.
- Study the governance structures of nonprofits in your organization's peer group and in your community, particularly those of nonprofits in the sectors of most interest to you (secondary education, higher education, health care, arts, social services, and so on).
- Learn about the expectations of board members in your organization, how these compare to the expectations of board members in peer organizations, how they have changed, and how they are being changed. Ask about what works and what doesn't work in initiating, implementing, and supporting increased expectations.
- Get as much time as possible in front of your organization's board and board committees. Get to know individual board members and what matters to them.

CHAPTER 5: THOUGHT PARTNER

- Read! Read what leaders in your organization are reading. Read what nonprofit leaders are reading. Read what donors are reading. Read what nonprofit leaders are writing. Follow authors who are important and influential in the nonprofit sector generally and in fields in which you work and expect to work—such as education, health care, the arts, or international relief.
- Study how your organization and other organizations present themselves in writing. Read mission and vision statements, case statements, and strategic plans. Identify elements and approaches that produce the most clear and compelling presentations.
- Read what donors say about their motivations for giving. See giving pledge.org for letters from many of today's top philanthropists.
- Ask your organization's major donors why they give.
- Give to other organizations, and think about the intellectual and emotional aspects of your decision about where and how much to give.

- Understand your bosses' perspectives and align your work as closely as possible to their approaches and their goals. Evaluate rigorously your chemistry with your boss and with other senior leaders, in order to be better prepared to evaluate the potential for chemistry with a future CEO boss. Work on putting yourself in the shoes of CDOs and CEOs for whom you work. Learn about the forces that come into play in their decision making.
- Identify the five influence leaders with the greatest potential to enhance or inhibit your boss's success. Identify the five influence leaders with the greatest potential to enhance or inhibit your success. Pay attention to how this group changes over time.
- Anticipate your boss's needs, get out in front of them, and stay in front of them.
- Be an "organizational sociologist." Study the culture of your organization, and get to know how organizational cultures develop and change. Be institutionally fluent, not just knowledgeable.
- Meet CEOs of other organizations and ask them what they most need and want from their CDOs.
- Be intellectually curious. If you don't know, ask; don't fake it.
- Practice empathy. Try to understand others' perspectives and motivations before criticizing. Improve your own openness to constructive criticism from others. Think carefully about the approaches of your critics, the approaches that work better than others, and why.
- Take at least one job working in a development shop considered "world class." Regardless of the level of job you hold, observe what is required for excellence. CEOs and board members seeking transformation of their development programs look for CDO candidates who know from first-hand experience what a leading program entails.
- Make sure that you're an interesting person. If your colleagues don't want to have lunch with you, why would you think a prospective donor would want to have lunch with you? Talking about fundraising is interesting only to a point. Well-developed personal and family interests make you a more compelling lunch or dinner partner.
- When you interview for a CDO role, seek a CEO with a vision you find compelling—a vision you can share and own.

CHAPTER 6: FLAG BEARER

- Be philanthropic. Find your passion and support it financially.
- Be a volunteer.
- Engage friends and family in supporting the organization you serve or organizations important to them.

- Read everything published about your organization.
- Reflect on your own level of intellectual and emotional engagement, and potential for that engagement, with your organization and with other non-profit organizations.
- Eat, sleep, and breathe the mission of your organization. Talk about it!
- Seek positions in organizations with missions and values that resonate deeply with you. Don't chase title and salary in any positions, including those prior to the role of CDO. If you love what you do, those will come. Without that love, the thrill of title and salary fades quickly.
- Know yourself well enough to understand whether your values and an organization's values will be in alignment. If not, you won't fit in, and you won't succeed.
- Build experience in shaping vision, adopting vision, translating vision into words you can own and sell, and promoting vision outside of your own area.
- Practice positioning your supervisor for success. Don't worry if your supervisor, or your supervisor's supervisor, gets credit for something you've done.
- Meet and read about leading, beloved philanthropists. Tell stories to your family and friends about philanthropists and their impact.
- Meet and learn from CDOs known as successful flag bearers.

CHAPTER 7: VISIONARY AND CONFIDENT SIGHT RAISER

- Practice positive thinking. Almost every glass is partly full and partly empty. Don't settle for the empty part, but don't dwell on it either. It is difficult if not impossible to carry negative thoughts about a task and convince others that the task is achievable.
- Set ambitious but achievable goals, and when energy wanes or optimism fades, rally the troops.
- Be proactive in goal setting and in raising your team's sights. At the same time, push back on goals that you do not believe are achievable.
- Bring well-researched alternative solutions to your supervisor when you bring problems or questions.
- Ask why things are done the way they are, and don't settle for WADIT-WAs (we've always done it that way).
- Develop a risk-taking attitude. Informed by the bigger picture, who the competition is, and what the trends are, look for opportunities, and try new things. Study innovation in the field, and bring ideas to your supervisor and your team.
- Study changes that work and changes that don't work. Especially for those that didn't work, find out why.

- Get to know successful change agents, and add at least one to your network of advisors.
- Seek out visionary leaders, and learn what goes into building strong vision. Create a vision that captures the imagination and loyalty of your team.
- If you don't have belief and confidence in your organization or its leadership, you aren't doing yourself or your organization any favor by staying.
- When seeking your next job, make sure you have a high level of belief and confidence in both the organization and its leadership. If your next role is a CDO role, it is essential that you have faith in the CEO and board leadership.

CHAPTER 8: TALENT MAGNET

- Be a problem solver. When you bring a problem to the attention of your supervisor, offer one or two possible solutions.
- Remain optimistic, and be known as an optimist.
- When others become agitated, practice restoring calm rather than feeding anxiety.
- Inject positive energy. Every member of a team either adds to the team's energy or detracts from it, and he or she makes that choice in every conversation, every day.
- Take great care in hiring. In the words of one CDO, "You can't fix dishonest, you can't fix stupid, and it's very hard to fix lazy." People who are hungry and driven work hard and inject important energy.
- Hire people who are so smart that you don't mind being the dumbest person in the room! Never settle for a less-than-excellent hire. Hire people who complement your skills and talents. Be confident enough to surround yourself with talented, intelligent people and be humble enough to listen to them.
- Never act as if you're the smartest person in the room in meetings with colleagues and board members. Part of your success has been demonstrating your intellect, knowledge, and experience. Now you will also be able to demonstrate your humility and willingness to learn. Monitor how much time you spend speaking versus listening in meetings; you will learn a lot more by listening. Consider yourself a perpetual student who can always learn much more. It will result in your becoming and being known as a thoughtful, wise, and strategic leader.
- Build networks of support within your organization, across the development profession, and with other nonprofit leaders. Make investments in the success of others.

- Attend meetings of your peers at peer organizations to make contacts and to learn about other successful approaches to development work.
- Don't confuse leadership with power. "Power is like a Chinese finger puzzle—the more you try to assert it, the more stuck you get," says Tim Child. Leadership is about providing direction, vision, and inspiration, and then leveraging the strength and power of your whole team.
- Lead by example. Model the behavior you want from your best employees.
- Don't throw anyone on your team under the bus—ever.
- Keep yourself and your team focused on principal objectives; avoid or minimize distraction and confusion.
- Discuss your career aspirations with your supervisor, and engage him or her if possible in helping you reach aspirations in your current position and beyond.
- Discuss the career aspirations of staff members who report to you, letting them know that you are invested in their career growth.
- When you receive a compliment for your work, immediately give credit to anyone and everyone who helped.
- Look out for colleagues who are struggling or discouraged. Offer some words of encouragement, or treat them to lunch.

CHAPTER 9: MENTOR TO FUTURE CDOs

- Gain experience outside your own areas of specialty.
- Observe CDOs. You can often learn just as much from a bad boss as from a good one, and you will learn from observing ineffective CDOs as well as effective CDOs, inside and outside of your organization.
- Be ready to learn, from everyone and anyone. View every constituent, internal and external, as a potential teacher or mentor.
- Identify people from whom you have a lot to learn, and take the initiative to keep in regular touch with them.
- Pay it forward—honor your mentors by taking the time to mentor others.

ADDITIONAL WORDS OF WISDOM

- Demonstrate your value by raising money—not by talking about it, but by doing it, both with partners such as a CEO or other organizational leader, and independently.
- Know what you don't know, and build at least a working knowledge of every area of advancement. Work in as many areas of advancement as possible before taking the top job. Don't get to the top job too fast.

- Know your strengths and weaknesses in the areas of people management, time management, life and work balance, and presentation skills. Go to a good executive coach.
- Obtain a broad skill and knowledge set in fundraising, management, operations, and strategy development. Successful CDOs are skilled fundraisers and managers, but also have a deep appreciation for development infrastructure. A program with underfunded or immature infrastructure cannot support even the best frontline fundraisers.
- Take a "number two" job before looking for a CDO position. It's a very different role from the CDO. Both are very important. Number two is often more of a daily manager, does not need to take the risks that a CDO does, and does not have the same exposure and vulnerability of the CDO. Some people find they like the role of number two best.
- Seek always to add value.
- Always do what you say you will do, and be known as a person who gets the job done—completely, correctly, within budget, and ahead of deadline.
- Never confuse activity with achievement. Be results oriented. Make things happen.
- Be willing to take on responsibilities "above your pay grade." Leaders often turn to people they've already observed doing the job. Don't shy away from an interim role. Inside candidates are often overlooked, but experience gained is always valuable.
- Avoid thinking, "That's not in my job description." Be someone known for creative solutions. Susan Paresky shares the following story: "I was asked to come to the home of a dean one Saturday morning to talk about putting together a dinner for a major prospective donor. The dean then asked if I would take charge of redecorating the living room and dining room to make sure it would be gracious and appropriate for entertaining. I ended up hiring a decorator and making the first floor of his home a very inviting and gracious space. He entertained beautifully and began to entertain faculty and students all year round. And we got the gift too!"
- Blossom where you're planted, and the next job will come. Looking for your next role and not thriving in your current role is a mistake. Paying more attention to where you're heading than to doing your best in the job you have leads to resentment, rather than support, from your colleagues.
- Don't lie.
- Don't go along to get along. Applying this simple phrase can be anything but simple. One CDO told a story of having to stand up to a president who insisted on spending the appreciation on restricted endowment gifts on a high-priority new project, stating his belief that the organization's only obligation to donors was the payout on the original gift amounts. Putting his job on the line, the CDO eventually had to go to board members and

seek their assistance in persuading the president to change his plans, thereby preserving the institution's integrity with respect to stewardship of endowment agreements, including the standard expectation of donors that appreciation on endowed funds stays with the endowed funds. Another CDO, charged with raising sights, advised a board chairman against accepting a naming gift at an amount that senior administrators agreed, and benchmarking clearly showed, was far below an appropriate level. Though the CDO made clear that the ultimate decision would be up to the board, the board chair never forgave the CDO, and when the president retired, the CDO was abruptly dismissed. The CDO paid a high price for doing his job with integrity. At the end of the day, you have to look at yourself in the mirror and be proud of what you see.

- Learn from CDOs you admire about how they allocate their time. Think about how you would allocate your time, and be prepared to discuss this up front with a potential CEO boss, so that expectations are aligned.

- Whenever you interview for a job, do your homework. Make sure you understand culture, finances, dependence on fundraising, makeup of the board, and aptitude for and commitment to fundraising among leaders. Do your own "feasibility study," measuring the potential for you to succeed given leadership, culture, expectations, and resources.

- Recognize that your greatest work will benefit people not yet born. Build your program for the organization's future and not just for today. See yourself as part of a continuum, and leave each program you manage stronger than when you left it. Don't put down your predecessors; build on their best work.

- Dress for the part. Err on the side of being the best-dressed person in the room. Personal appearance has a significant impact on overall impression. Many CDOs also recommended developing the ability to give CEOs and other internal leaders advice on appearance and presentation. A great deal of trust is required, and the need for tact cannot be overestimated!

- Constantly upgrade social sophistication. Learn proper etiquette for a variety of social settings. Read a good book on executive etiquette.

- CDOs serve at the pleasure of CEOs, and successful CDOs never lose sight of their support role. Remember that a big part of your job is to make your CEO successful.

- Do what you love, and love what you do. Volunteers and donors give time and financial resources with no paycheck whatsoever. Life's too short to devote long hours to a development position that doesn't produce some reward beyond a paycheck.

Appendix C

Hiring Guide for Organizations

There are many great CDOs, many great organizations, and yet many bad "marriages." "Leadership is contextual, situational," says Daniel Porterfield, president of Franklin & Marshall College. "Organizations need the right development leader at the right time."

The following questions are designed to help everyone involved in the hiring of a CDO achieve a more comprehensive, fulfilling, and lasting fit for the organization.

UNDERSTAND YOUR NEEDS

- What were the qualities of past CDOs that the organization most wants to find in the next CDO, and what qualities of past CDOs do they wish to avoid?
- What skills, talents, and experiences are most needed at this time? In what areas is deep expertise required, and in what areas can the organization afford a steeper learning curve?

UNDERSTAND THE CANDIDATE

- Is the candidate a proven frontline fundraiser, capable of leading other fundraising staff by example?
- Is the candidate a proven leader, someone you would want to follow?

- Does the candidate readily give credit to others—donors, colleagues, staff members—or do they in their resume, writing, and verbal communications tend to describe achievements in the first person?
- Has the candidate built strong relationships internally and externally? Can they give an example of collaboration with a colleague outside development that resulted in a significant win for their organization?
- Do they view donors as philanthropic partners and use language that reinforces that view? Can they readily describe such a partnership, where organizational objectives and donor objectives were brought into a highly productive alignment?
- Has the candidate demonstrated proficiency with financial and strategic planning? Can they describe their involvement and impact on their own organization's planning or on that of an organization on whose board they serve? Can they describe how different types of fundraising revenue, such as unrestricted gifts, gifts to endowment, and pledges, are recorded in financial statements? Can they articulate the principal financial challenges and opportunities of the organization and its sector?
- Has the candidate served on an advisory or governing board? Can they describe the contributions a CDO is expected to make to recruitment and engagement of board members? Do they and the organization agree on the role the CDO plays in the nominating process?
- Is the candidate prepared to be an effective thought partner to the CEO and other key leaders? Does the candidate understand the organization's mission, key competitors, sector, and key challenges? Do they have intelligent questions and observations? Do key leaders want to spend more time with the candidate, discussing issues beyond fundraising? Would the candidate be an interesting dinner guest?
- Is the candidate persuasively passionate and knowledgeable about the organization, its mission, its vision, and its values? Can they tell a story about why the organization matters to them, personally? Do they support the organization or similar organizations as a volunteer or donor?
- Does the candidate convey a sense of confidence in the future of the organization? Is the candidate capable of raising the sights of the interviewer, even in the interview itself? Can the candidate give examples of raising the sights of a staff member, of a colleague, and of a donor?
- Does the candidate have a strong track record of attracting and retaining high-performing staff members?
- How does the candidate describe their most important mentor, and their favorite mentee?

Appendix D

Guide for the CDO Candidate

CDO candidates need to do their own "mini feasibility study" to determine whether they can be successful in an organization, before assuming the role of CDO. Given the limited time candidates generally have with CEOs and board members during the search process, making such a determination is difficult. Here are some suggestions:

- Study the organization chart to figure out how and where philanthropy fits.
- Ask about how the organization's leaders will measure the CDO's success. Look for widespread consensus, and where it does not exist, probe more deeply.
- Ask about the previous CDO's greatest strengths and weaknesses, especially to learn about how others view the role, not just the person in the role.
- Talk to others who have held the position along with consultants who have worked with leaders in the organization.
- Assess your own professional trajectory, including where you've been and where you're headed. Will the organization's challenges and opportunities allow you to build on past experience and achieve professional goals? For example, if success requires program overhaul, is that your strength, and is that what you most want to do? If success requires focus on a handful of top prospective donors, is that where you want to spend your time, and will you have or be able to build the infrastructure you need to manage day-to-day operations? If success requires substantial hiring and program growth, do you have the skill, talent, and drive of an entrepreneur and

builder? How large is the staff, and how does the balance between administration and fundraising required square with your own strengths and
desires? What is the balance between short-term and long-term revenue
needs, and will that balance allow you to do your best work?

- Assess your potential for chemistry with the CEO and other key leaders.
  Will it be enjoyable to spend significant time with them traveling, at
  dinners, and in meetings?
- Ask the organization's donors about the philanthropic culture. Ask them
  about their relationships with the CEO and other key leaders, about their
  relationships with other donors, and about the way the development staff
  treats them. Identify red flags, and satisfy yourself that changes you believe necessary can be made. For example, if stewardship is a problem, do
  organizational leaders know it's a problem and want to correct it?
- Determine the degree to which you will participate in financial planning,
  strategic planning, and board growth. Ensure that you will have access to
  people and meetings that will allow you to make your best contribution.
  For example, if significant increase in the overall capacity of the board is
  required, will you have sufficient input to the nominating process?
- Study all the financials and prepare to ask questions that relate to finances.
- Be sure to speak with board members. The search process provides an
  excellent opportunity to begin relationships with board members. Those
  involved in the selection of a CDO typically feel more responsibility for
  helping the CDO get off to a good start. An absence of board members in
  the search process is a potential red flag.
- Determine the potential for thought partnership between you and other
  leaders, especially the CEO. Use every possible resource to learn about the
  CEO's vision, values, and management style. If a search consultant is
  involved, ask that person about his or her interactions with the CEO and
  about how others describe their work with the CEO. Learn about the
  CEO's track record in hiring and retaining direct reports, at the organization and in prior jobs. Ask everyone you meet during the search process
  about the CEO. Read what the CEO has written and view videotaped
  speeches and interviews with the CEO on the organization's website and
  elsewhere.
- Study other organizational decision makers and power brokers in similar
  ways.
- Think carefully about your own passion for the organization's mission,
  vision, values, and leadership. Is it sufficient to inspire others and to
  sustain you in challenging times?
- Assess the CEO's and other key leaders' passion about the organization,
  its mission, its vision, and its values. Do leaders convey a sense of belief
  and confidence in the future of the organization? Will they be sufficiently
  inspiring to donors? If belief and confidence are low, is there a sufficient

number of influential people with passion to assist you in instilling passion in others?

- Determine the level of belief and confidence in both the organization and its leaders among development staff members.
- Most organizations hiring new CDOs are looking for growth in fundraising results, and growth usually requires change—change in personnel, change in approach, change in level of budget allocated to the development program, and perhaps change in board capacity and willingness to play a leadership role in fundraising. Test whether key decision makers are prepared for, and will be supportive of, change. If you believe substantial increases in program resources will be required, make sure you are confident before you accept the position that those resources will be made available.
- The CDO can't be the only sight raiser. If the organization wants sights significantly raised, will the CEO be an effective partner in doing so? Are there enough other potential partners?
- CDOs are only as good as their teams. Is the right team in place? Will you be able to make changes? Will you have sufficient resources and discretion to hire the people you will need to complement your skills and make you successful?
- Finally, go where you are confident you can make an important contribution to the organization and, at the same time, to your own professional growth and fulfillment. Each step requires a leap of faith, but do sufficient research in advance to be reasonably certain you are the right person in the right place at the right time.

Appendix E

Individuals Interviewed for The Chief Development
Officer: Beyond Fundraising

I interviewed the following individuals between December 2012 and April 2013. Interviews lasted between 30 and 90 minutes. I conducted 14 in person and the remainder by telephone.

Christine Adams, director of development, Phillips Academy; former senior associate dean, Harvard University Kennedy School; former interim vice president of development, Beth Israel Deaconess Medical Center; former interim vice president of resources, Wellesley College

Karen Alexander, vice president for development, Chicago Symphony Orchestra; former senior vice president for development and external affairs, Loyola University Health System

Andrew Alper, chair, University of Chicago board of trustee; co-chair, development committee, Mount Sinai Medical Center; trustee, University of Chicago Medical Center

Paige Bartels, vice president for external relations, Bennington College; former director of development and external affairs, Homes for the Homeless

Mercedes T. Bass, chairman of the board, Fort Worth Symphony Orchestra; vice chairman, Metropolitan Opera board of directors; vice chairman, Carnegie Hall board of trustees; vice chairman and chair of the development committee, American Academy in Rome board of trustees; chairman, American

Friends of Covent Garden; chairman, Friends of European Sculpture and Decorative Arts, Metropolitan Museum of Art

Deborah Breen, president, Aspen Valley Hospital Foundation; former executive director, Northern Dutchess Hospital Foundation

Alex Brose, vice president for development, Aspen Music Festival and School

Helen Brown, president, The Helen Brown Group

J. Timothy Child, vice president of institutional advancement, The J. Paul Getty Trust

Nim Chinniah, executive vice president for administration and chief financial officer, University of Chicago

Karl Clauss, vice president for development and alumni relations, Swarthmore College

Jared Cohon, president, Carnegie Mellon University

Carmen Creel, director of development, Philbrook Museum of Art

James Cuno, president, The J. Paul Getty Trust

James Digan, president, Rochester General Hospital Foundation; former executive vice president for development and chief advancement officer, The Children's Hospital of Philadelphia

Matthew Eynon, vice president for advancement, Franklin & Marshall College; former executive director of university advancement, University of Massachusetts–Lowell

Susan Feagin, special advisor to the president, Columbia University; former executive vice president for university development and alumni relations, Columbia University; former vice president for development, University of Michigan

Alan Fletcher, president, Aspen Music Festival and School

Maya Gasuk, senior associate, West Wind Consulting

Mary Lou Gorno, trustee, Chicago Symphony Orchestra; trustee, University of Chicago

Jon Gossett, vice president and chief development officer, St. Luke's Episcopal Health System; former vice president and chief development officer, Planned Parenthood Federation of America; former senior vice president, development, American Public Media Group; former executive director of development and executive vice president, Houston Grand Opera Association; former director of development, The Guthrie Theater Foundation

Joan Harris, chair emerita, Harris Theater for Music and Dance; past chair, Aspen Music Festival and school board of trustees

Randy Helm, president, Muhlenberg College; former vice president for College Relations, Colby College

Tom Herbert, vice president for university advancement, Miami University

Beth Herman, principal, EBH Consulting, LLC; former vice president for college advancement, Washington College; former vice president for college advancement, Franklin & Marshall College

Timothy Higdon, consultant and adjunct assistant professor, George H. Heyman Jr. Center for Philanthropy and Fundraising; former chief of external affairs, Girl Scouts of America; former deputy director for external affairs, Amnesty International USA

Marylou Houston, philanthropy director, Children's Hospital Colorado Foundation

Margaret Hunt, vice president of development, New York Public Radio

Robert Hurst, chair, Aspen Music Festival Board of Directors; co-chair, Whitney Museum Board; chair, Aspen Institute Development Committee

Patricia "Trish" Jackson, executive director of College and Foundation Partnerships, Fullbridge Program; former vice president for advancement, Smith College

Anne Johnson, vice president for development, San Francisco Symphony; former development director, The Lawrence Community Theatre

Kassandra Jolley, vice president for institutional advancement, Spelman College; former vice president of university advancement, Roger Williams University

Ann Kern, senior client partner, Korn/Ferry International

Kelly Kerner, senior vice president for development and alumni relations, Bowdoin College; former vice president for college advancement, Bates College

Rod Kirsch, senior vice president for development and alumni relations, The Pennsylvania State University

Ann McLaughlin Korologos, chair, board of trustee, Anderson Ranch Arts Center; former chair, board of trustee, RAND Corporation; former chair, board of trustee, The Aspen Institute

Robbee Baker Kosak, vice president of university advancement, Carnegie Mellon University; former vice president for advancement, Rensselaer Polytechnic Institute; former vice president for development, Bucknell University

Mark Kostegan, senior vice president for development, Mount Sinai Hospital; former chief development officer, Brigham and Women's Hospital; former senior vice president for development, Joslin Diabetes Center; former vice president for development, Children's Hospital Boston; former vice president for development, Massachusetts Eye and Ear Infirmary; former vice president for development, Winchester Hospital; former vice president for development, Melrose-Wakefield Hospital; former vice president for development, Saint Anne's Hospital

Constance Kravas, vice president, university advancement, and president of the foundation, University of Washington; former vice chancellor for university advancement, University of California–Riverside; former vice president for university advancement and president, Washington State University Foundation

MaryJane Kubler, founding partner, KublerWirka

Harry Lester, president, Eastern Virginia Medical School

Reynold Levy, president, Lincoln Center for the Performing Arts; former president, AT&T Foundation

Ken Manotti, vice president for alumni relations and development, University of Chicago; former vice president, institutional advancement, The American University in Cairo

Bruce Matthews, vice president, Campbell & Company

Jerry May, vice president for development, University of Michigan; former vice president for development and president of the Foundation, The Ohio State University

Jane McAuliffe, president, Bryn Mawr College

Peter Meinig, chairman emeritus, board of trustee, Cornell University; former chair, committee on alumni affairs and development, University of Tulsa

Robin Merle, vice president and chief development officer, Hospital for Special Surgery

Carol O'Brien, president, Carol O'Brien Associates, Inc.; former director of university development, Cornell University

Susan Paresky, senior vice president for development and The Jimmy Fund, Dana-Farber Cancer Institute; former vice president, Brandeis University; former associate dean for development, Harvard School of Public Health

Daniel Porterfield, president, Franklin & Marshall College

Don Randel, president, Andrew W. Mellon Foundation

David Ressler, president, Aspen Valley Hospital

Cecile Richards, president, Planned Parenthood Federation of America

Jesse Rosen, president and CEO, League of American Orchestras

Riccardo Salmona, vice president for development and public affairs, The Juilliard School; former vice president, external affairs, World Monuments Fund; former deputy director, American Folk Art Museum

Sandy Sedacca, vice president and chief development officer, Planned Parenthood Federation of America, and vice president and chief development officer, Planned Parenthood Action Fund; former vice president for development, John F. Kennedy Presidential Library Foundation; former dean of development and external relations, Harvard Graduate School of Education; former national director of development, American Civil Liberties Union

Robert Sharpe, president, Sharpe Group

Scott Showalter, vice president of development, Los Angeles Philharmonic

Curt Simic, president emeritus, Indiana University Foundation; former vice Chancellor for development and president of the University of California–Berkeley Foundation; former vice president for University Relations, University of Oregon; former director of development and alumni affairs, University of Tennessee Center for the Health Sciences

James Thompson, senior vice president and chief advancement officer, University of Rochester; former executive director of development and college relations, Lindenwood College

David Unruh, senior vice president, Grenzebach Glier & Associates; former senior vice president for institutional advancement, Temple University

Laura Walker, president and CEO, New York Public Radio

Susan Washburn, principal, Washburn & McGoldrick, Inc.; former vice president for University Relations, St. Lawrence University; former vice president for administration and advancement, The Evergreen State College; former vice president for development, Centenary College

Adam Weinberg, president, Whitney Museum

Nancy Winship, senior vice president of institutional advancement, Brandeis University; former vice president for endowment and development, Combined Jewish Philanthropies in Boston

Elizabeth Boluch Wood, vice president for development, Princeton University; former chief development officer, The Cancer Institute of New Jersey

Darrow Zeidenstein, vice president, resource development, Rice University

Robert Zimmer, president, University of Chicago

About the Author

Ronald J. Schiller began his development career in the late 1980s at his alma mater, Cornell University, one of the largest and most mature development programs at the time. Prior to joining the development office, as associate director of choral music at Cornell, he raised money for the women's chorus and men's glee club to take concert tours. After he played a lead role in raising $250,000 for a concert tour of Asia, the development office took notice and invited him to join the staff.

In the University Development Office, he served first as assistant director, then as associate director, then as acting director of development for the College of Arts and Sciences, and finally as major gifts officer. During those years, as the university undertook higher education's first-ever campaign over $1 billion, Cornell's development staff grew from fewer than 100 to over 300. Ron was fortunate to work with and learn from some of the most highly regarded development professionals in higher education, including and especially Jean Gortzig, Dick Ramin, Inge Reichenbach, and Dave Dunlop.

In 1994, Ron assumed his first senior management position in fundraising at the University of Rochester's Eastman School of Music, where he grew a small staff of three to ten. As the head of a school-based program within a large university, he experienced some of the roles and responsibilities of a chief development officer (CDO) without taking them all on at once. He participated in organizational financial planning, budgeting, and strategic planning, but his responsibility stopped short of supporting a governing board. He worked with multiple constituencies with competing priorities, but with a university vice president to guide him and back him up.

When the director of the Eastman School left to become president of New England Conservatory, he recruited Ron to join him at the conservatory as vice president for institutional advancement, Ron's first comprehensive CDO role. From there, Ron's career took him to larger and larger shops, including Northeastern University, Carnegie Mellon University, and the University of Chicago, where as vice president he led a team of over 450 staff members that completed a $2.38 billion campaign, established the university's principal gifts program, and helped the university secure its first two nine-figure gifts.

Ron served as president of the National Public Radio Foundation, leading the development of a national fundraising strategy focused on donors and their overall connection to public radio, a strategy that required a significant increase in the collaboration between NPR and its several hundred independent member stations. In the first year of a principal gifts program established by Ron and his colleagues, NPR had as many seven-figure-gift donors as it had had in all forty previous years combined.

He then served as senior vice president for business development at Lois L. Lindauer Searches, assisting the firm in expanding its CDO search practice.

Ron has served on many boards and advisory councils, including the Cornell University Council, the Cornell University Trustees' Glee Club Advisory Council, the Harris Theater for Music and Dance Board of Trustees, the Buddy Program Board of Directors, the Cayuga Chamber Orchestra Board of Directors, the Board of Trustees of the North Carolina School of the Arts, the American Academy in Rome Development Committee, the American Friends of Covent Garden, the Salt Bay Chamberfest, and the Mendelssohn Choir of Pittsburgh Board of Directors.

Ron serves as founding partner of the Aspen Leadership Group (www.aspenleadershipgroup.com) and the CDO Career Network (www.cdocareer.net) created to provide support and community for current and aspiring CDOs. His numerous ventures in the social profit sector bring him into daily contact with chief executive officers, board members, and CDOs. He is a regular speaker at conferences on the role of CDO and has co-chaired the Council for Advancement and Support of Education's Winter Institute for Chief Development Officers.